HARVARD REMINISCENCES

HARVARD

REMINISCENCES

BY

ANDREW P. PEABODY, 1811-1893

Essay Index Reprint Series

BOOKS FOR LIBRARIES PRESS
FREEPORT, NEW YORK

First Published 1888
Reprinted 1972

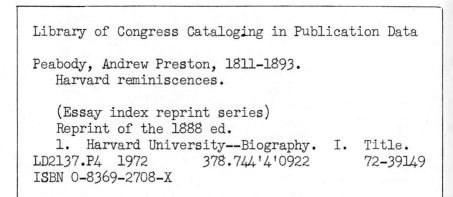

Library of Congress Cataloging in Publication Data

Peabody, Andrew Preston, 1811-1893.
Harvard reminiscences.

(Essay index reprint series)
Reprint of the 1888 ed.
1. Harvard University--Biography. I. Title.
LD2137.P4 1972 378.744'4'0922 72-39149
ISBN 0-8369-2708-X

PRINTED IN THE UNITED STATES OF AMERICA
BY
NEW WORLD BOOK MANUFACTURING CO., INC.
HALLANDALE, FLORIDA 33009

PREFACE.

My purpose in this book is to give my reminiscences of the college officers whose names appeared with mine in the several annual catalogues in which I was registered as undergraduate, theological student, and tutor. Of some of these men I have very little, of others much, to say. Much of what I tell, I saw and heard: the rest was derived from authentic sources of information. I undertake this work mainly because it ought to be done, and there are few who are old enough, yet able, to do it. There were, sixty years ago, associated with the several departments of the University, men who ought not to be forgotten, yet of whose worth and services there remains no record except in the fading memory of their few surviving pupils, as whose self-appointed representative I write. I have adopted the order of graduation for my sketches, which embrace fifty-six years of college-age, from 1776 to 1831 (inclusive).

To these biographical notices, I have appended a chapter containing some of my reminiscences of Harvard College as it was during my novitiate as a student.

CONTENTS.

HARVARD REMINISCENCES.

AARON DEXTER.

(1776.)

THIS was the only name on the catalogue in my college days that bore the then rare and almost mysterious title of *Emeritus*, which Dr. Dexter retained for thirteen years, after having filled the chair of Chemistry and Materia Medica for thirty-three years. In his time chemistry was almost an unknown territory, while the field of *materia medica* was immeasurably large; drugs and (so-called) specifics having been not only in more ample use, but employed in a very much greater variety, than in the practice of the present day. Dr. Dexter was chosen to office in 1783, — the year after the formation of the Medical School. His professorship was unendowed until 1790, when William Erving, moved by affection for Dr. Dexter, his physician and friend, left a thousand pounds, the income thereof to be applied to the increase of the salary of the Professor of Chemistry. Hence the name of the Erving Professorship now held by Professor Cooke. In 1816 Dr. Dexter tendered his resignation, which was accepted with a vote recognizing "his good services to the cause of science, and his zealous attachment to the interests of the University."

HENRY WARE.

(1785.)

Dr. Ware was born in Sherborn, Mass., in 1764. His father was a farmer; and, till his father's death in 1779, he performed on the farm such labor as was not beyond his strength, with no intermission except attendance at a ten-weeks' winter school. He once told me that he nearly lost his life in what, half a century ago, was still called "the great snow,"—a storm, which, in rapidity and depth of snowfall, had not then been equalled within the memory of man. He had ridden to mill for his father; and on his return, with the impediment of heavy meal-bags, he and his horse were so far buried in the snow, that he was extricated with difficulty, and hardly alive.

I first saw Dr. Ware when he examined me in the Greek Testament, on my admission to college. I was then profoundly impressed by his paternal bearing and manner, and by the rare blending of sanctity and sweetness in his deportment. He thus in my early boyhood won my affectionate reverence; and in after-years, when I was associated with him in the college Faculty, and a frequent visitor at his house, I revered him none the less, and could hardly love him more.

tiful boy, ten or twelve years of age, in his arms. It was a son of Dr. Ware. He took the child at once, held him while the physician, who had been summoned, ascertained that there was no hope of recovery, and then superintended the arrangements for his conveyance home. Through the whole he was perfectly self-possessed, and yet exhibited an absolutely motherly tenderness; and his aspect during that hour of agony has constantly recurred to my remembrance, as indicating the intensest parental feeling, only the more vividly manifest for his undisturbed calmness and serenity. On the following Sunday he appeared as usual in the pulpit, but not as usual with one of those lectures which seemed to us so dry and wearisome. He preached from the quaint text, "I will work; and who shall let it?" The sermon, in composition and delivery, seemed a rehearsal of the scene by the river-side. It made no parade of feeling,—no direct reference, indeed, to the event so fresh in our minds. It was a touching statement of the baffling and appalling mysteries of the Divine Providence, with the simplest expression possible of trust in the wisdom and mercy which it transcends the capacity of man always to trace and verify,—the whole so phrased and uttered as to make it evident that it represented the very processes of thought and feeling by which he had schooled his own heart to faith and submission. It was an eminently logical sermon, and, as a mere scholastic exercise, fully equal to the most subtile of his dogmatic discussions, but at the same time tremulously full of emotion, all the more appreciable by eye and ear, because controlled and chastened.

Dr. Ware's lectures, though otherwise heard with indifference, furnished his college name; for of course every college officer had (and probably still has) his nickname. The tradition was, that in earlier days Dr. Ware had been called "General Scope," from the frequent recurrence of that phrase in his lectures.[1] But in my time he was called "Sykes," or "Dr. Sykes," after Archdeacon Sykes, whose works he often quoted.

He heard us recite in Butler's "Analogy," in Paley's "Evidences," and, I think, in Paley's "Moral (or immoral) Philosophy." In these exercises, after the then established fashion, he gave no instruction, but simply asked questions, and marked on a numerical scale of eight his estimate of the answers. In our senior year he gave us a short course of lectures on the contents and history of the Bible, covering the ground occupied by the (so-called) Introductions to the Old and New Testaments. These lectures were remarkable for their comprehensiveness, thoroughness, and perspicuity,

[1] He was said to have learned of this appellation from seeing pasted on the door of his lecture-room a large caricature of himself on horse-back in military attire, with a negro attendant behind him; the two figures being labelled respectively, "General Scope" and "Tenor."

It was not uncommon among the students humorously to impugn his veracity, on the ground of the marvellous frequency with which, in conversation, lecture, and sermon, he said, "I am not *a-ware*."

and especially for the accuracy of their definitions. They contained a large amount of valuable knowledge that might otherwise have not fallen within the reach of those who did not pursue expressly theological studies. I well remember the stress which he laid on the distinction between the genuineness and the authenticity of a book or document, — a distinction sometimes lost sight of by men who ought to know better.

In the Divinity School Dr. Ware was again my teacher. His course extended through three years, and embraced the evidences and doctrines of natural and revealed religion, with a survey of the great moments and salient topics of church history. Here his method, as it seems to me, was pre-eminently wise in the division of labor between teacher and pupils. His exercises were held weekly, and generally exceeded two, sometimes three, hours in length. He gave us each week the next week's subject, in a series of questions, with a list of reference-books. We each of us wrote a full dissertation on the subject. In the class-room the professor called upon one of us to read all that he had written, on the next to read whatever he had that differed from or added to the first paper, and so on through the class. At the close Dr. Ware commented on our essays, supplied what we had omitted, and, if the subject was one as to which there could be difference of opinion, presented both sides of the question at issue with such perfect impartiality, that one who did not previously know could hardly have ascertained which was his own side, while those of either party would have been ready to adopt his statement of their case.

The authorities that we consulted were for the most part English divines of established fame for learning and ability; but, as I recall the titles of their books, there is hardly one of them of which our younger theologians have ever heard. They are, most of them, master-works of their kind; and they have lost their value, not because of any defect in them, but because the ground of discussion has been so entirely changed that the questions then rife are either definitely settled, or by common consent ignored. They are like the Russian sentinels that kept faithful watch and ward, night and day, on the site of a fortification half a century after it was demolished. Should the slumbering controversies ever be re-awakened, Sykes and Douglas, Soame Jenyns and Leland, Farmer and Watson, will be found at their post, and the truth could need no more stalwart or better armed champions.

Dr. Ware was three times married, and was the father of nineteen children, most of whom lived to hold conspicuous and honored places in professional life or in society, and to verify in their children, and their children's children, the beneficent law of heredity. His family discipline must have been, almost beyond precedent in his time, gentle and mild. I heard him say that in his large family he had never seen the need of the rod, or of severe punishment of any kind. In two or three instances he had quelled fits of anger by hydropathic treatment, which must have been of enduring benefit; as rigid self-control was characteristic of all those of his children who attained years of maturity.

ISAAC PARKER.

(1786.)

CHIEF JUSTICE PARKER, of the Supreme Court of Massachusetts, was Royall Professor of Law from 1816 to 1827. He was the first professor of law in the University. The Law School was established in 1817 at his suggestion. He never bore an active part in its administration, though it undoubtedly had the benefit of his advice and influence. The income of the Royall Professorship was barely sufficient to pay for a course of twelve or more lectures to each successive senior college class. Judge Parker's course comprised such facts and features of the common and statute law as a well-educated man ought to know, together with an analysis and exposition of the Constitution of the United States. His lectures were clear, strong, and impressive; were listened to with great satisfaction, and were full of materials of practical interest and value. He bore a reputation worthy of his place in the line of Massachusetts chief justices; and the students, I think, fully appreciated the privilege of having for one of their teachers a man who had no recognized superior at the bar or on the bench.

JOHN THORNTON KIRKLAND.

(1789.)

President Kirkland was the son of Rev. Samuel Kirkland, for many years missionary to the Indians in Oneida County, N.Y., — a man of rare ability, dis cretion, and tact in his work, and so much beloved by the tribe under his charge, that their chief, in dying, begged to be buried by his pastor's side, that they might rise together on the judgment-day. The two graves may still be seen side by side. The son had also a goodly heritage of mind and character from his mother, — a niece and foster-child of the elder President Wheelock. In his early childhood the future president received a kick from a horse, which left a lifelong indentation in his forehead, in shape not unlike a horseshoe. He entered college at the age of fifteen. The next year he enlisted — probably with other students who have left no record of their service — in the army raised for the suppression of the Shays Rebellion. He graduated with high honor in 1789, was for two years a college tutor, and was ordained as pastor of the New South Church in Boston in 1794.

Dr. Kirkland's church had among its worshippers a large number of men in high position, and of the leaders of society; and he, from the first, held a foremost place, equally as a preacher, and as a man of broad and various culture, of social gifts and accomplishments, and of superior practical wisdom. He had, too, a rich vein of the wit which bears the close kindred to wisdom indicated by the common root of the two words. With him a *bon mot* often did the work of a homily, and more efficiently. It was said that when a country deacon called on him for advice about a quarrel that had sprung up in his church, concerning the dogma of "the perseverance of the saints," he replied, "Here in Boston we have no difficulty on that score: what troubles us here is the perseverance of the sinners." Of his early professional reputation we find one signal token in the degree of D.D., conferred on him at Princeton, when he was only thirty two years of age, — a distinction the more remarkable, as he was well known to belong to the liberal school of theology.

On the death of President Webber, in 1810, Dr. Kirkland was designated as his successor by the unofficial choice of the community, and was duly elected before the close of the year. Probably no man ever held office in a literary institution with so entirely unanimous respect, admiration, and love, on the part of his pupils. He knew them all; and, with few exceptions, he knew all about them, and about their parents; for Harvard College then drew a much larger proportion of its students than now from its immediate neighborhood. He examined the successive classes, on their admission, in Virgil's "Georgics;" but his scrutiny was directed much more to the countenance, the family traits, and the indications of character, than to the tokens of scholarship; and a face thus seen was never forgotten; so that he not only always addressed students by name, but recognized them, and could recall their college standing and history, even after the lapse of many years. He took a fatherly interest in every member of college, and was on the watch for occasions when there might be need of advice or warning, which was always so given as to make it seem a privilege to have received it. In all important cases of discipline he communicated the votes of the Faculty, and always in such a way as to impress the offender with his kindness, to wound his self-respect as little as possible, and to start the resolution for better conduct in future. There were instances in which the interview with him, in receiving a sentence of suspension, was a turning-point in the student's course as a moral being; and the cases were not rare in which the youth who went to receive his sentence in a mood of insolent bravado, crept back to his room to hide his tears.

The president knew, also, the length of every student's purse; and there were not a few who completed their course solely by his aid, unasked, and sometimes when it was impossible to learn how he became aware of the need. I can recall from my own knowledge several cases of men who attained no little distinction, — among them a president of one of our principal colleges, — who were prevented from leaving college in debt and in despair, by the thoughtful and unsolicited kindness of Dr. Kirkland, whose espionage was as vigilant and keen for the needs, as was that of some of his associates in the Faculty for the misdoings, of the students. As his charities were large, and his resources small, he may have been, to a considerable degree, the almoner of others: but he certainly gave of his own all that he could; for with no family to provide for, and no expensive habits, he was no richer when he resigned his office than when he graduated, forty years before.

With all Dr. Kirkland's kindness, he had a marvellously quick and sharp eye for trickery and falsity. It was not easy to impose upon his good nature. Students were obliged to apply to him for leave of absence; and, if the alleged excuse was one manufactured for the occasion, he never failed to detect the fraud. He generally granted the leave desired in such instances, but always with some droll, half humorous remark, which indicated his understanding of the case, put the applicant to shame, and made him reluctant to proffer a like request again, even if there were good reason for it. I doubt whether a student ever dared to go to him a second time with one of the falsehoods then not condemned in the college code of ethics, — though I trust that, under the present *régime*, in which students are treated as gentlemen, amnesty is no longer given to untruths under any pretext.

On Sundays Dr. Kirkland generally preached once, — in the afternoon, if I remember aright; and his sermons were listened to with interest and admiration, and that rather for the structure, meaning, and point of each successive sentence, than for any continuous course of thought or reasoning. He preached almost always on the ethics of daily life: and his sermons were made up for the most part of epigrammatic, proverb-like utterances, gems of the purest lustre, alike in diction and in significance, but, if not unstrung, strung on so fine a thread that only he could see it. Indeed, we had a strong suspicion that his sermons were put together on the spot. He used to carry into the pulpit a pile of loose leaves, from which he was visibly employed in making a selection during the singing of the hymns. I doubt whether he often, if ever, wrote a whole sermon after he came to Cambridge. The law that underlies the arithmetical rule of "permutation and combination," gave him, in a limited number of detached leaves, an unlimited number of potential sermons. His voice was pleasant and musical; his manner in the pulpit, grave and dignified; but it was commonly quite evident that he felt less interest in his preaching than his hearers did. Yet there were occasions on which he manifested deep feeling, and rose into an eloquence which can hardly have been surpassed in the meridian of his fame as a preacher. After a death in college or in one of the college families, in any crisis of public affairs, and at the opening and the close of the college year, he chained the rapt attention of his audience, and was intensely impressive.

On one occasion, after a series of disturbances almost amounting to a rebellion, in which all the classes were concerned, he preached on the text, "O my son Absalom! would God I had died for thee," making a profoundly touching appeal to the students in behalf of their parents, and telling them what sorrow and shame they were bringing upon their homes by conduct which must issue in their separation from the college in disgrace. Never was a sermon heard with more solemn interest, and never was one more efficient. Order was restored at once, and on Monday morning a deputation from all four classes called on the president to ask for a copy of the sermon for the press. His reply was somewhat in this wise: "You, students, last week gave me little time to write. But I found a sermon of Robert Walker's that met your case; and, were I to print my sermon, there would be more quotation-marks than you or I would like to see."

In all probability, Dr. Kirkland's reason for writing so little for the pulpit, was not the indolence with which he was charged, and which was probably inferred from his manner in public and in private when there was no special need of energy, but the constant pressure of official cares and duties which, with absolutely no clerical assistance, devolved wholly upon him, and in which there was no remissness or procrastination. The mere correspondence made necessary by his position, limited, indeed, by the slowness and cost of the mail-service, must have imposed no light burden. His reluctance to perform needless pen-work may be illustrated by an anecdote which I believe to be authentic. For an edition of the writings of Fisher Ames, he had engaged to furnish a prefatory memoir. The book was printed; and the publisher waited week after week for the memoir, which was always on the point of being written. At length certain friends of both Mr. Ames and Dr. Kirkland came to the president's house one morning, and told him that they would not leave the house till they could take the memoir with them. He at once applied himself to the work; and the result was a monograph, not only perfectly adequate and satisfactory, but so rich, graceful, and racy in style, that it might at this day be brought forward as a model, rarely equalled, of pure, classical English composition.

Dr. Kirkland officiated, I think always, at daily evening prayers, the morning service being conducted by the other members of the Faculty in turn. His scriptural reading was as nearly like his preaching as he could make it, very often from the Proverbs or the ethical Psalms; when from the New Testament, from precept or parable, rather than from narrative. His prayers impressed us with their uniform solemnity, and, on special occasions, with their fervor. There was never any thing about them that seemed formal or perfunctory; but, while their language was always such as might have indicated careful elaboration, his whole manner made us sure that he was not rehearsing a prayer, but voicing the sincere devotional feeling of the passing hour.

Dr. Kirkland's personal presence, always dignified and graceful, became on important occasions absolutely august and majestic. No one that witnessed it could ever forget his reception of Lafayette in front of University Hall, and his presentation of the assembled students to the illustrious guest. It was probably the grandest moment of his life, and it is impossible to over-estimate the lifelong impression which he made on all who saw and heard him. Years afterward Lafayette spoke of this as having transcended all similar ceremonies in his honor.

Dr. Kirkland seemed to all of us an old man, and the most venerable person that we knew or could imagine. I belonged to the last class that received their degrees at his hand, and he was then but fifty-six years of age. Before the next commencement, he had a stroke of paralysis, which led to his resignation. He recovered a certain degree of bodily vigor, but not his elasticity of mind or his capacity of labor; and it was impossible to recognize in the conversation — sensible, courteous, and kind, yet without any distinctive mental quality — of the elderly gentleman of ease and leisure, the traits which had made him one of the most brilliant of men, the life of society, to listen to whom had been an inspiration and a joy.

Shortly before Dr. Kirkland's resignation, he married Miss Elizabeth Cabot, who induced him to make with her an extensive tour in the South and West of this country, and then to spend three or four years in sojourn and travel in Europe, Egypt, and Palestine. But neither her assiduous care nor the stimulating influence of new scenes and experiences was of avail in restoring the powers that had been benumbed by disease. On his return, he lived for the most part in Boston; and, until the last year of his life, there was no further decline in health of body or of mind. He died in 1840, after a few months of growing infirmity, and but a single week of disabling illness.

STEPHEN HIGGINSON.

STEPHEN HIGGINSON, by three months Dr. Kirkland's junior, his parishioner and intimate friend, was the son of an eminent Boston merchant of the same name, and a descendant of the first minister of Salem, whose posterity have in every generation been distinguished for ability, enterprise, civil service, and philanthropy. The younger Stephen Higginson was for many years a successful merchant in Boston, and was especially remarkable for his generosity in every direction in which he could hope to do good. He was commonly called "the man of Ross," — a title of honor not then so trite as it has since become, and a not unfit designation of a man who regarded all that he had or gained, as an open fund for every cause and every person that needed and deserved his aid. After many years of prosperity he sustained heavy losses that induced him to retire from business. In 1818 he was entered as "Steward and Patron" on the list of college officers. The steward then performed not only the work which now belongs to the bursar, but the greater part of what was actually done of that appertaining to the treasurer. The treasurer, then an unsalaried officer, chosen for his high position in the community, and not for his financial ability, received and disbursed the college funds, and retained in faithful custody evidences of property, bills and vouchers, but kept, and probably could have kept, no regular set of books; and whatever of book-keeping there was, fell to the province of the steward, who needed such financial skill as Mr. Higginson could bring to the office. Whether his position as patron was a sinecure, I think was never known. If there were any students to whom he stood in that relation, they would have been ashamed to confess it. But it was a law of the college, mandatory in form, in fact only permissive, that parents who lived at a distance from the college should commit such spending-money as they might allow to their sons to the care of the patron, who should superintend its expenditure, and receive a certain percentage on the funds thus disbursed. If any income was ever derived from this source, it was probably less than a like charge on the expenditure of a single rich student might be now.

Mr. Higginson took a most generous interest in the Divinity School, of which he was the veritable "patron." He watched the building of Divinity Hall as carefully as if it had been his own dwelling. The theological students were always his welcome, and often his specially invited, guests. He made contracts for text-books, and never failed to be present at the unpacking of books from abroad; and I well remember his consternation on finding every copy of an invoice of Hebrew Bibles, as he supposed, misbound, with the titlepage at the end of the book. He kept up a correspondence with vacant parishes, and knew the qualities and adaptations of the candidates for settlement so thoroughly, that his advice was of much more value to a church than any judgment that could be formed on a probation of three or four Sundays. Many of the happiest settlements in the ministry were made through his kind agency.

Over and above all, it was a pleasure to see and know Mr. Higginson, — with a countenance always glowing with benevolent sunshine, manners so genuinely those of a finished gentleman that they seemed the accumulated growth of the two centuries of gentle culture in his family, speech as genial in tone as it was always kindly in substance, and rapid, because his words of greeting and good cheer seemed to trip one another up in their haste to find utterance. He was both before and behind his time, — before it, in the warmth of his sympathy and the breadth of his charity; behind it, in the courtliness and refinement which belonged to the born aristocracy of an earlier generation.

JOSIAH QUINCY.

(1790.)

Mr. Quincy had a more intense and efficient will-power than any other man that I ever knew. He combined the sturdy uprightness of purpose and strenuousness of action which are commonly — I will not say how aptly — termed Roman, with the pure and high ethical standard, and the generous regard for human well-being, which are distinctively Christian. He was, by nature and by hereditary right, of the genuine aristocracy, born to rule; and, could the world's governing and care-taking be in the hands of men of his type, there would be no yearning for democratic institutions. With few exceptions, he accomplished whatever he undertook, notwithstanding the frequent dissent, at the outset, of colleagues or advisory boards; and the result always verified his prescience, and justified his action. No man can have encountered and overcome more opposition than he, and no old age was ever richer than his in honor and in gratitude; and this as well from those who had sought to obstruct him in his life-work, as from those who had been in full sympathy with him. In what he deemed a righteous cause, he would have stood in a minority of one against the whole world; and the universe held not the price for which, in word or deed, he would have swerved one hair's-breadth from his integrity.

Mr. Quincy was a pioneer in opposition to the

slave-power, and a few months before his death he wrote to President Lincoln that the subject had occupied his mind for more than seventy years. When first a member of the Massachusetts Legislature, he took the lead in a movement toward procuring an amendment of the article in the Constitution of the United States which includes three-fifths of the slaves in the basis for representation in Congress; and at that early period he predicted the internecine conflict with slavery, of which he lived just long enough to be assured of the successful issue. His whole Congressional life was an unceasing protest against overwhelming majorities, — often against Southern encroachments and aggressions, and most emphatically against those measures, with reference to Great Britain, which culminated in what every one must now admit to have been a needless war. Afterward, when he was again in the Senate of Massachusetts, and a vote of thanks to Captain Lawrence, for the capture of the "Peacock," was sent up from the Lower House, he procured its replacement by the resolution, "That in a war like the present, waged without justifiable cause, and prosecuted in a manner indicating that conquest and ambition are its real motives, it is not becoming a moral and religious people to express any approbation of naval and military exploits, not immediately connected with the defence of our sea-coast and soil." Ten years later this resolution was expunged by a strictly party vote of a Democratic Senate; but the man who moved this measure, and engineered its passage, in after-years repented of his action, and was wont to express his earnest wish that it were possible to restore the mutilated record.

For a little while Mr. Quincy was judge of the Municipal Court of Boston; and with characteristic independence, when he did not find law in accordance with his sense of right, he made it, and in one signal instance made it for the whole English-speaking world. Down to his time the English and American courts had acquiesced in the common-law doctrine, that the truth of an alleged libel could not be admitted in defence on a criminal charge, and in the maxim, "The greater the truth, the greater the libel." Joseph T. Buckingham, well known as an editor, for his fearless exposure of hypocrisies, pretensions, and frauds, had published articles injurious to the character of Rev. John N. Maffitt, then the most popular of Methodist preachers. Maffitt, relying on the law as it had always been understood and administered, procured Mr. Buckingham's indictment for libel. Mr. Quincy, in open defiance of all authority save that of reason and justice, ruled that the defendant should be permitted to prove the truth of his allegations, and that the publication of the truth, with good intentions, and for a justifiable end, was not libellous. Under this ruling, the defendant was acquitted; and Maffitt, though sustained by the *esprit de corps* of the Methodist clergy, never recovered a righteously ruined reputation. The principle involved in Mr. Quincy's ruling is now recognized equally in our own and in the mother country.

Mr. Quincy was chosen mayor of Boston the second year of its incorporation as a city, and for six successive years. He organized every department of the civil service then required, on a system for the most part retained to the present day, and where changed, changed for the worse. Under his auspices, a large district between Beacon and Cambridge Streets, deemed an unassailable den of the vilest depravity, and in which even the life of a respectable person was not safe, was entirely cleared of its foul occupancy, and some of the best streets of the city now cover what was a seething dunghill of filth and crime. The Faneuil-hall Market, commonly and very fitly called by Mr. Quincy's name, is a monument of his official enterprise. It was built from the proceeds of the land made by filling in the flats on which it was erected, the residue of which was covered at once with warehouses that have always paid a heavy tax; and besides its invaluable worth for its purpose, it is in itself an important source of revenue to the city.

Mr. Quincy abolished the entire system of municipal feasting at the public charge, and instead thereof invited the office-holders of every grade, in suitable numbers and at proper intervals, to his own table. He lost his seventh election — with a large plurality, but not a majority, in his favor — by the hostility of the body of firemen which he had created, and which craved for their chief a man whom he regarded as unfit for the place.

Just when the city of Boston concluded to dispense with services from which it is still deriving no little benefit, Harvard College was in urgent need of a president. The presidency, for more than a century, and with but a single exception from the very first, had been held by a clergyman. At this time, however, Dr. Ware, who filled the office provisionally, was the only prominent clerical candidate; and he, though well fitted for the charge, was six years older than Dr. Kirkland. Besides, it was on some accounts very desirable that a man largely versed in the management of funds and of material interests should be put at the head of the college. Under Dr. Kirkland the college had, indeed, grown richer, because his popularity had attracted givers and gifts; but the income had fallen short of the expenditure. What was sometimes called the Salem administration, — a *régime* financial as well as literary, — had now come into power. Judge Story and Dr. Bowditch, both of them Salem men, were leading members of the corporation; and they had added to the Board as treasurer, Ebenezer Francis, a native of Beverly, hard by Salem, and had employed Benjamin R. Nichols, another Salem man, for a full year, in examining the accounts of preceding years, ascertaining accurately the financial condition of the college, and starting a set of books which have since been kept as those of every corporation should be kept. At the same time, Charles Sanders, a Salem man, was made steward. Meanwhile the interior affairs of the college craved an executive head. They could not have been better managed than they were by Dr. Kirkland, and the few able, wise, and experienced professors, who, with him, constituted almost the whole Faculty, and virtually had the control of the institution. Their careful deliberation and sound judgment had supplied the lack, and in some respects had done more than the work, of system. But they were already dropping from the list by reason of infirmity or death; and younger professors, and with larger classes an increased number of tutors, were soon to hold the ascendency in all matters of government and discipline.

These were among the chief reasons for the election of Mr. Quincy as Dr. Kirkland's successor; and the college had, and still has, ample reason to rejoice in his administration. He at once brought his practical wisdom and enterprise to bear upon all its outside interests; and he established an interior system, which needed very little change for many years, and has of late required gradual modification rather than reconstruction to meet the enlarged and multiplied demands of an institution, in its means, opportunities, and breadth of generous culture, as far transcending the Harvard College of 1829 as did that, the infant seminary under Dunster and Chauncy.

Among Mr. Quincy's earliest reforms at Cambridge was one bearing no remote analogy to his work as mayor in cleansing the vice-infested district of West Boston. Harvard College was, as is well known, in its birth and purpose, a religious institution; and pious citizens of Boston used to send their slaves to Commencement for their religious instruction and edification. But the negroes soon found that they could spend their holiday more to their satisfaction, if not more to the good of their souls, on the outside, than in the interior of the meeting-house. When this discovery was made, the service was attended with ever-increasing interest on the part of the sable population, and with exercises adapted to their receptivity, till at length Commencement came to be the great gala-day of the year for the colored people in and about Boston, who were by no means such quiet and orderly citizens as their representatives are now, while their comparative number was much greater. When I entered college, the entire Cambridge Common, then an unenclosed dust-plain, was completely covered, on Commencement Day, and on the nights preceding and following it, with drinking-stands, dancing-booths, mountebank shows, and gambling-tables; and I have never since heard such a horrid din, tumult, and jargon, of oath, shout, scream, fiddle, quarrelling, and drunkenness, as on those two nights. By such summary methods as but few other men could have employed, Mr. Quincy, at the outset of his presidency, swept the Common clear; and during his entire administration, the public days of the college were kept free from rowdyism.

Mr. Quincy effected improvements, which in some respects were almost creative, in the exterior condition of the college. The college-yard had, on his accession to office, hardly half its present area. He made with the First Parish of Cambridge an arrangement by which the old church-edifice, near the present site of Dane Hall, and the very ancient and unsightly parsonage-house — long disused for its original purpose — adjacent to the Dana house, were surrendered to the college; and instead thereof, on land that had been occupied by two dilapidated wooden dormitories, there was built, at the cost of the college, a church, which was made the property of the parish, with the reservation of the right of use on Commencement and other public days, and the tenancy of certain gallery-pews which were occupied by professors and their families during vacations, — easements which must by this time have lapsed by non-user. By this transaction the college obtained the control of nearly the entire space now called the college-yard; though there were still two other old houses between the president's house and the Dana house, both then occupied by professors, but removed when they became vacant. While the new church was in progress under the president's immediate direction, he superintended and hastened the building of Dane Hall for the Law School, which was now dislodged, having had its previous quarters in the lower story of one of the demolished dormitories.

Among Mr. Quincy's favorite enterprises and

achievements was the establishment of the Astronomical Observatory. Previously there had been a small telescope, unmounted, kept with the scanty apparatus belonging to the department of physics, and taken out for two or three evenings each summer to show Saturn's rings to the senior class. In 1839 Mr. Quincy made an arrangement, by which Mr. William Cranch Bond, then in the employ of the United-States Government, removed his instruments to Cambridge under an appointment as Astronomical Observer to the University. The Dana house was secured for the purpose, a revolving dome was erected for the telescope, and a transit instrument adjusted in the meridian line, with a small tower on Blue Hill in Milton for its point of sight. Not long afterward Mr. Quincy obtained, in great part by personal solicitation and by the prestige of his influence, the funds requisite for the building and equipment of the present Observatory, which was hardly completed when he resigned the presidency, but which continued to be among the foremost objects of his special interest during the residue of his life, and to which he gave ten thousand dollars as the foundation for a publishing-fund.

The suitable housing of the college library was another object of Mr. Quincy's early and successful endeavor. In the last century all the books but one in the library had perished in the burning of Harvard Hall; and the present Harvard Hall, though its second story had more than room enough for the

determined. There was before his time no uniform system of registration for class-work. Each teacher kept his record in his own way, or, if he saw fit, relied, without record, on his own memory and judgment. College honors were conferred by vote of the Faculty, without any documentary evidence on which the vote could be based. The older professors had, indeed, acquired a judicial skill, or tact, so that their decision commonly received the assent of students who were not themselves disappointed; but there were frequent instances in which individual students thought themselves sorely aggrieved, while there was in recent memory one signal instance in which the highest honors of a class had been unfairly won, and erroneously conferred. Mr. Quincy devised in all its details a system by which a student's daily record should constitute his due and fitly earned place in the scale of rank or merit. Every recitation was marked on a scale of eight, and every theme or written exercise had some multiple of eight for its maximum. From the sum formed by the aggregate of these marks, there was a specific deduction for every unexcused absence, and every college censure. The number thus standing against each student's name represented the estimate in which, by the blended ratio of scholarship and character, he deserved to be held as a member of the college, and as a candidate for its beneficiary endowments or its honors. The aggregate was so formed as to leave hardly any room for even unconscious favoritism:

while as it grew rapidly, and amounted to several thousands, it seemed impossible that any two should hold the same place; though this happened in one instance, in which two first scholars were bracketed in the rank list, and marked as of equal standing in the Commencement programme.

Mr. Quincy presided over the administration of this system. Some one member of the Faculty kept the accounts, and the president audited them. I held this charge for a year: and every Tuesday morning I carried my book, and the separate lists from which I had made my entries, to his office; and he went over them with me as carefully and minutely as if the most momentous interests were at stake, leaving no doubt, that, had he found me inaccurate, he would have relieved me at once, and laid the burden on other shoulders. This system remained unchanged through the three administrations next succeeding his, and with very slight changes during the two next following; and its underlying principles are still recognized, though its specific methods, for obvious reasons, are no longer practicable.

Mr. Quincy, also, labored earnestly and persistently to establish it as a rule and a principle, that the students of Harvard College should be held amenable to the civil authority for crimes against the law of the land, even though committed within academic precincts. The habits of the students were rude; and outrages, involving not only large destruction of property, but peril of life, — as, for instance, the blowing up of public rooms in inhabited buildings, — were occurring every year. In the endeavor to subject the students to the municipal law, Mr. Quincy was sustained by the governing boards of the college, but encountered an untold amount of hostility and obloquy from the students, their friends, and the outside public. He persevered, and gradually won over the best public opinion to his view. The principle is still admitted, and I cannot but think that it ought to be practically recognized with regard to all forms of misconduct that are punishable outside of the college walls. While the detestable practice of hazing was rife, crimes that were worthy of the penitentiary were of frequent occurrence, resulting, in some cases, in driving a persecuted freshman from college; in many instances, in serious and lasting bodily injury; and once, at least, in fatal illness. The usual college penalty punished the parents alone. The suspended student was escorted in triumph on his departure and his return, and was the hero of his class for the residue of his college life. I remember an instance in which a timid freshman had his room forcibly entered at midnight, his valuables stolen, and a bucket of cold water poured upon him as he lay trembling in his bed. Had the perpetrators of that crime been certain that, in case of detection, they would be indicted for burglary, and punished by a year or two of imprisonment, they would no more readily have broken into a freshman's room than into a jeweller's shop. The kindest possible course toward the students themselves would be to make them liable to all the penalties of the laws which they are often tempted to violate. The matter is of no concern whatever to at least nineteen-twentieths of a class. As to the remaining twentieth, strict amenableness to the law would save almost all of them from excesses and disorders which have a baneful influence on their characters, it may be, for the remainder of their lives.

In his intercourse with the students, Mr. Quincy lacked the suavity of address that had distinguished his predecessor, but possessed no less of genuine kindness. He was abrupt, almost harsh, in manner. He seldom remembered a face; and when a student — even one sent for but a few moments before — entered his study, he was encountered by the question, "What's your name?" So much was this his habit, that if it so happened, in a rare instance, that he did recognize a countenance, he was more likely than not to say, "Well, Brown, what's your name?" But he knew intimately well the character, history, and belongings of the individual students, as their names stood in the catalogue; and his constant aim with regard to them was, not only to do justice, but to show that mercy which is the better part of justice. I well remember one instance, which is but a specimen of many, in which he averted an impending sentence of suspension from a student, on learning that his mother was in so critical a condition of illness that her son's disgrace might be more than she could bear; and I am glad to add that the censure, then not unmerited, was cancelled by a blameless and exemplary life from that day to this.

Mr. Quincy sought, so far as was possible, to relieve the rudeness of the barrack life to which students were then subjected by the isolation of the college, and by the rules which forbade absence from town except on Saturday. For the greater part of his presidency his house was open for one evening every week or fortnight, with a hearty welcome to such students as would be his guests, and with music, attractive society, and the most hospitable attention on the part of the ladies of his family.

On public occasions Mr. Quincy maintained not only the dignity and grace, but also the prestige of classical culture, that appertained of right to his office. At his own inauguration, at that of new professors, and at other seasons of public solemnity, he delivered Latin addresses, as to the authorship of which I know nothing, yet which bore some internal tokens of his own composition. Thus, in stating the amount of Dr. Dane's endowment of the Dane Professorship of Law, he designated "dollars" as *nummi nostræ reipublicæ*, — not bad Latin, yet that of an American statesman rather than of Dr. Beck, our then newly appointed German professor of Latin. Mr. Quincy's greatest occasion was the two-hundredth anniversary of the founding of the college, in 1836, when he delivered the commemorative address, which was the nucleus of his subsequent two-volume history of Harvard College. In this, as always, he showed himself the master of an English style, pure, rich, and vigorous. His elocution, when he had a manuscript before him, retained, with the weight and impressiveness, the fervor which had marked his eloquence in deliberative assemblies; but he no longer, if ever, sustained the even flow of unwritten discourse. When he felt the most strongly, his words seemed at first to be struggling for utterance, and then were poured out in spasmodic jets, with prolonged intervening pauses.

Mr. Quincy probably never looked forward to any official duty with the reluctance with which he submitted to the necessity of receiving Andrew Jackson as President of the United States, and conferring upon him the degree of doctor of laws. Party feeling was then intense beyond all recent experience, and Jackson was held in abhorrence by all who did not worship him. I was in the college Faculty at the time, and I think that he had not a single admirer on the Board. Preparations for a public funeral — certainly for his — could not have been made less cheerfully than ours for his welcome. We all, however, put the best face upon what we could not shun, and escorted our guest to the chapel. Francis (now Professor) Bowen, the first scholar in the senior class, delivered a Latin oration. Mr. Quincy then conferred the degree in an elegant Latin address. The general replied, probably in English,[1] but in so low a tone that it was impossible to know what he said. He was then escorted to the president's house, where the ladies and gentlemen of Cambridge were presented to him. His whole bearing, in the chapel and in the drawing-room, by its blended majesty and benignity, won for the time the reverence and admiration of all who saw him. Ladies brought their children to him, that they might have a lifelong remembrance of his kiss. His strongest political opponents rendered to him their cordial homage. Had his re-election been pending, however it might have been on the morrow, there would on that day have been not a single vote against him. Those who, like Mr. Quincy, most dreaded his coming, regarded him ever afterward with the respect which he certainly merited by his integrity of purpose and his patriotic services, if not by the wisdom of his administration.

Mr. Quincy lived to be the oldest graduate of the college, and sat for his photograph with four success-

[1] Charles Augustus Davis, who, under the pseudonyme of "Major Jack Downing," wrote for The New-York Commercial Advertiser a burlesque journal of Gen. Jackson's Northern tour, said that, while Mr. Quincy was making his address, the general asked him (Jack Downing) how he should reply, and was advised to recall to memory all the Latin that he had ever heard. In compliance with this suggestion, his response was, "*E pluribus unum, — Ne plus ultra, — Sine qua non.*"

ors in office. He retained to the last his love of the college, rendered to it every service within his power, and ceased to be present on its public days only when prevented by disabling infirmity. He exceeded his ninety-second year, with some failure in mental activity and in the memory of recent events, but with unimpaired clearness and strength of mind, and richly endowed with those traits of the spiritual nature which merge the late evening shadows of life in the dawn of the eternal day.

LEVI HEDGE.

(1792.)

THOSE who remember the elder Dr. Hedge, are constantly reminded of him by his son, Rev. Dr. Henry F. Hedge. The son closely resembles the father in face, but with more force and variety of expression; in voice, but with greater strength of utterance and flexibility of modulation; in form, but with a larger frame. The father, who was our professor of logic, metaphysics, and political economy, was exact and punctilious to the last degree; but, in an equal degree, just and kind in his relations to the students. Few of us saw him except in the class-room; but when a legitimate indulgence or an act of clemency was desired, we went to no college officer more readily than to him: and in his study his rigidness of manner disappeared. In the recitation hour he imparted no instruction whatever, and gave us distinctly to understand that he regarded the words of the text-book as preferable — and undoubtedly they were — to the best paraphrase that we could make of them. Students expected to gain his permanent good will and lasting favor by reciting his "Logic" *verbatim*, and there were myths afloat as to his own laudation of the book: "It took me fourteen years, with the assistance of the adult members of my family, to write this book; and I am sure that you cannot do better than to employ the precise words of the learned author." But I never could find the person who had heard any thing of this kind; and — unfortunately for the tradition — the book was published in the sixth year of his professorship, before there were any adult younger members of his family.

We read our forensics to Dr. Hedge; and we had reason to be very thankful to him for the generous range of subjects assigned to us, and for his elaborate, wise, and — when there was need — learned summing up of the arguments on both sides of the question. We had also with him what he chose to call "voluntary discussions," generally on subjects of political economy, in which, in default of willing, he drafted unwilling, disputants, and of which his weighty closing words were the only instructive portion.

An attack of paralysis closed Dr. Hedge's official life, in 1832. He was partially restored, and in his retirement enjoyed twelve years of quiet and serene old age.

If Dr. Hedge thought well of his "Elements of Logic," he was entirely in the right. While I held the Plummer Professorship, I took charge for several years of the department of logic. At that time, I examined all the text-books that I could find; and in point of method, comprehensiveness, and diction, Hedge's is by far the best. It lacks some few details that are incorporated into later treatises, as also the illustrative diagrams, which are very serviceable. But, if I were to make a manual for college use, I should be glad to retain every word in this treatise, and should want to make very few additions to it. There is not in the whole book a definition, or the statement of a principle or a rule, that would bear abbreviation, and that would not lose by being amplified. The first sentence and the closing paragraph deserve to be quoted, the former for its perspicuity, the latter for its practical wisdom.

"The purpose of Logick is to direct the intellectual powers in the investigation of truth, and in the communication of it to others."

"The student should remember, that neither learning the best rules, nor reading the best models, can supersede the necessity of intent and continued reflection. He should dwell on the operations of his own mind, and mark the difficulties, which prevent his arriving at clear conclusions; whether they arise from misapprehension of the subject, from the ambiguity of language, or from the biasses of association. He will insensibly form a logick for himself, which while it embraces the rules common to all minds, will be peculiarly adapted to the improvement of his own."[1]

JOHN SNELLING POPKIN.

(1792.)

Dr. Popkin, after a tutorship in Cambridge, was settled as a minister in the Federal-street Church in Boston, succeeding Dr. Belknap, and having Dr. Channing for his immediate successor. He retained his charge only three years, and resigned it against the wishes of his parishioners, on account of his own modest estimate of his ability to maintain so prominent and important a position. He shortly afterward became pastor of the First Church in Newbury, whence, in 1815, he was recalled to Cambridge as professor of Greek. His Newbury parish had a considerable proportion of men and families of superior intelligence and culture, and he was held in the highest esteem as a preacher there and in all the neighboring towns. Many of his sermons were printed; and they are not only among the best of his time, but decidedly in advance of his time, equally in

[1] Two or three years ago, the Faculty of a Roman-Catholic college in Canada instituted the inquiry whether there remained any copies of Hedge's Logic that could be procured for class use. The ground of preference was not, as it might well have been, its superior merit, but the fact that there was no more modern treatise that did not furnish among its examples of "fallacies" specimens of the accustomed reasoning of the champions of the Romish Church.

breadth and in depth of thought. He was also an assiduous and devoted pastor, and had the profoundest respect and love of his congregation. I well remember the tokens of undiminished reverence and honor manifested there at his death thirty-seven years after the close of his ministry, and the impressive eulogy of his character and ministry then pronounced by his successor, the late Rev. Dr. Withington.

Dr. Popkin was a bachelor, and for many years led a very lonely life. It was said that he had in his early days been strongly attached to a lady whose affections were bestowed elsewhere; and it is certain that when she died, in his old age, he sent for a carriage, and attended her funeral, though he had not been a wonted visitor at her house, nor, indeed, in any house. Till near the close of his professorship he lived in a college-room, for most of the time in the second story of Holworthy. He at first boarded in the college commons: but, finding the dining-hall too noisy and tumultuous, he after a little while took his meals in his own room; the venerable Goody Morse cooking his food, bringing it to him at the regular college hours, and in various ways taking the most assiduous care for his comfort. Shortly before he resigned his office, a widowed sister and two orphan nieces of his came to Cambridge; and he established himself as the head of their family, in the old Wigglesworth house, which stood next to the president's house in Harvard Street. He afterward built a house on the North Avenue, adjacent to a house then recently built by his classmate and lifelong friend, Dr. Hedge. The two ex-professors used to hold the most pleasant intercourse on their several sides of the dividing fence, but neither ever entered the other's house; as Dr. Popkin, while the kindest of men, and social in his way, neither made nor invited visits.

Dr. Popkin was undoubtedly the best Greek scholar of his time; and there is a mine of recondite learning stowed away in his edition of the Gloucester Greek Grammar, and in the notes in the American edition of Dalzel's "Collectanea Græca Majora" signed "P," and generally, with his characteristic modesty, pointed with an interrogation-mark, though no one was better entitled than he to employ the affirmative form of statement. I can hardly say that he gave instruction in the recitation-room, though he muttered in what seemed a breathlessly rapid soliloquy a great deal that would probably have been instructive, could it have been heard and understood. The criterion of a good recitation with him was not grammatical knowledge, but the accuracy and elegance with which the Greek was rendered into English. He had at the same time a singularly delicate ear for the detection of a rendering which was not the student's own; and, though he seemed to see very little, if a printed translation was brought in, he was not unlikely to discover and confiscate it. In like manner he accumulated a little library of interlined "Majoras," which had been made with assiduous care, transmitted from class to class, and held at a high price in the college market. But the students who cared little for the Greek language or literature could appear reasonably well at very small cost. He commonly called up the members of a division in alphabetical order, and one could always determine within a few lines the passage which he would have to construe. Once in a great while, however, Dr. Popkin would spread consternation by striking midway in the seats; but those who on such occasions utterly failed, felt entire security for many subsequent days. Those of us who really studied our whole lessons had a wearisome task. There was no Greek-English lexicon attainable. Our chief dependence was on the often inadequate Latin definitions of Schrevelius, and we were not sufficiently good Latin scholars not to need the mediation of a Latin dictionary between the Greek and the English. There were in my class two or three copies of the more copious lexicon of Hedericus; and round one of these half a dozen of us would sit, each with his Schrevelius, depending, when he failed us, upon the fuller supply of Latin meanings in the larger vocabulary. Under such difficulties, the actual amount of Greek scholarship fell far short of the estimate which it had in the professor's generous credulity.

Dr. Popkin would have had a majestic presence, had he so chosen. He was tall, with a massive frame, with a broad and lofty brow, and with features indicative of superior mental power. But shyness and solitude gave him an aspect and manners more eccentric than can easily be imagined in these days, when, under the assimilating influence of modern habits, idiosyncrasies have faded out, and every man means and aims to look like every other. His dress, indeed, was, in an historical sense, that of a gentleman; but his tailor must have been the last survivor of an else long extinct race. He never walked. His gait was always what is termed a dog-trot, slightly accelerated as he approached its terminus. He jerked out his words as if they were forced from him by a nervous spasm, and closed every utterance with a sound that seemed like a muscular movement of suction. In his recitation-room he sat by a table rather than behind it, and grasped his right leg, generally with both hands, lifting it as if he were making attempts to shoulder it, and more nearly accomplishing that feat daily than an ordinary gymnast would after a year's special training. As chairman of the parietal government, he regarded it as his official duty to preserve order in the college yard: but he was the frequent cause of disorder; for nothing so amused the students as to see him in full chase after an offender, or dancing round a bonfire: while it was well understood that as a detective he was almost always at fault.

Oddities were then not rare, and excited less surprise and animadversion than they would now. The students held him in reverence, and at the same time liked him. His were the only windows of

Dr. Popkin took his turn in officiating at the daily college prayers, and his peculiarities of manner were almost always merged in the sacred dignity and the profound solemnity with which he conducted the service. While in his own soul it was evidently the utterance of sincere devotion, and not mere routine, there were certain phrases, scriptural for the most part, that recurred so often as to attach themselves indelibly to my memory of him. Thus, among his ascriptions of gratitude, he seldom failed to offer thanks for "wine that maketh glad the heart of man, and oil [*ile*, as he pronounced it] to make his face to shine, and bread which strengtheneth man's heart," — wine having not yet fallen under the ban of even the Society for the Suppression of Intemperance, of which he must have been a member, as were the president and most of the Faculty. In the chapel service Dr. Popkin was apt to falter and hesitate, and even to sink into an unconscious bathos, when there was any thing unusual in the occasion, especially at the close or the beginning of a term, when he in vain attempted to embody the home-going or the re-assembling of the students in the stately phraseology which he was wont to employ. He seldom preached in the chapel; but on the rare occasions on which he supplied the president's place, he plainly showed that the pulpit was the fitting fulcrum for his life-power. He was a heedful listener to sermons, and a wise and discriminating critic. Some of us younger college officers sat with him on he came to this country on one or another of the many occasions on which worthy citizens of France found it desirable to emigrate. He was said to have a provincial pronunciation, and was therefore supposed to have been not a citizen of Paris. As to this, I can bear no testimony; for I was never his pupil. If I had been, I should not have known whether or not he conformed to the Parisian standard. He married the daughter of a deceased Cambridge clergyman, and was worthily held in high regard in Cambridge society. When I was in college, though he still had an almost youthful vivacity of speech and manners, his white hair denoted mature, if not venerable, age. He was always dressed with great precision, had his hair powdered, and was never without a profuse sprinkling of powder on the back of his coat. His English diction was correct in the choice of words, though intensely French in the utterance: and he certainly showed strong Anglican proclivities in the selection of his patron saint; for he hardly ever made an affirmation without sanctioning it "By George,"—the only expletive that ever garnished his conversation.

It was probably never known how good a teacher Mr. Sales could have been, if he had had teachable pupils. But the modern languages then formed no part of the college curriculum. They were extra and voluntary studies, and were not taken into the account in determining a student's rank. Of pupils in Spanish, Mr. Sales had only now and then one who expected to need the language for some practical purpose. His French classes were large, but were composed mainly of students who sought amusement rather than instruction, and whose chief aim was to impose on his long-suffering good-nature, and to put him to his wit's end in the vain endeavor to preserve some show of discipline. When I was tutor, my room in Hollis was adjacent to his class-room; and I never found his recitation-hours propitious for quiet study. Two or three times he invited my aid in restoring, or, to speak more correctly, in establishing, order, which lasted while I staid; and the few moments during which I sat while he proceeded with his class-work gave me my only personal knowledge of it. My relations with him were always pleasant, and were renewed unexpectedly but a short time before his death. It was in Portsmouth, on a summer morning. I was sitting at my writing-table, with open windows, and was startled by hearing "By George!" in a voice which, once heard, could not fail to be recognized. I sprang up, and ran to the door, and found Mr. and Mrs. Sales brought to a sudden stand by seeing my name on the door-plate. They spent a half-hour with me, and resumed by the next train the journey on which they had paused for the night. I am glad to remember that, otherwise than with most of his Cambridge coevals, his long life closed with no protracted period of enfeebled health and suspended activity.

JAMES JACKSON.

(1796.)

No man can ever have been more worthily loved and honored than Dr. Jackson; and such was the charm of his character, such sweetness, such benignity, such spontaneous kindness, such diffusive charity, that, if two superlatives can be compared, the love transcended the honor. Moderate in all things, he made the mean, which in a feeble man is contemptible, veritably the golden mean, and raised moderation from the weakness which it often is, to a supreme place among the virtues. Without pretending to do so, he practised the mind-cure; for his presence was always a power, and the patient must have been in a desperate case who did not feel the benefit of his visit before he followed his prescription. Indeed, the prescription was the least part of his ministry; for he was a pioneer sceptic as to the use of drugs. In practice he anticipated by many years the theories of Sir John Forbes and Dr. Bigelow, and made it his chief work to watch and, if there were need, to subsidize the curative energy of nature in disease. My personal acquaintance with him was slight; but it was my privilege to officiate at his funeral. A privilege I deemed it; for his many years of unsurpassed activity and usefulness had been followed by a condition of such infirmity and suffering, that those to whom he was unspeakably dear rejoiced in the assurance that "the mortal had put on immortality."

ing of the Revolutionary war, and is commemorated for pre-eminent worth as a public servant, a citizen, and a Christian. Asahel Stearns inherited his worth, his ability, and his high place in the esteem and reverence of the community; and the elaborate eulogy, which leaves no trait of merit unrecorded, on the father's gravestone, might have been transcribed in full on a memorial-tablet for the son. In 1817 the Law School of Harvard University was established; and Mr. Stearns, who had previously practised law in Chelmsford and Charlestown, and had represented the Middlesex District in Congress, was placed in charge of it, as the sole resident professor, which he continued to be till his resignation in 1829. The law-students were very few, and but twenty-six took the degree of Bachelor of Laws during his term of office. This does not mean that he failed to prove himself an able and desirable teacher, but simply that Mr. Stearns's office, which was the School, while it might furnish more direct instruction, afforded less opportunity for conversance with the practice of the law than offices in Boston. A building, a library, and an organized faculty, were essential to make the School attractive; and, even when these were supplied, the average number of graduates for several years did not exceed five. Professor Stearns was regarded as second in legal learning to no man of his time. He published a work on "Real Actions," which gave him reputation; and he was one of the commissioners for revising the Statute Law of Massachusetts. He was warmly interested in the public charities of his day, exercised a generous hospitality, and was equally respected and beloved. He was a man of grave and serious aspect and demeanor, but by no means devoid of humor, and was a favorite in society. His wife was a lovely woman, full of good works; and there was never a sick student in college whom she did not take under special charge, even watching with him by night, superintending all that was done for his relief and comfort, and, in his convalescence, feeding him from or at her own table till he could return without loathing to the coarse fare of Commons' Hall.

Professor Stearns was one of those terete men, in whose moral nature there are no prominences, simply because there are no depressions; who therefore leave a blessed memory, without specific details to be remembered. I have, however, one reminiscence of him which I like to recall, and am glad to record. When I first went to the White Mountains, it was in a stage-coach with Mr. and Mrs. Stearns, two young collegians, and two other young persons, their friends and mine. The eighth passenger was an elderly clergyman of a type now happily extinct, but which my older readers may recognize, — of that class of men who thought it their duty to vilify nature, and to treat contemptuously the beauty and grandeur of the outward universe. It ought to be said that he was not on a journey of pleasure, but on a mission from a certain anti-Catholic association which threatened great things, but had a very brief and inefficient life. As we reached one after another of the grand points of view on our route, my young friends were jubilant with delight and admiration, while our clerical companion glowered and growled in his corner. At length, when we came in full sight of Mount Washington, and there was a spontaneous shout of rapture, he exclaimed, as angrily as if he had been personally insulted, "How mean and paltry must all this be in the eyes of Him who weighs the mountains in scales, and the hills in a balance!" Professor Stearns rejoined calmly and reverently, in Pope's couplet, —

"'To Him no high, no low, no great, no small:
He fills, he bounds, connects and equals all.'"

JOHN COLLINS WARREN.

(1797.)

THE Medical School was organized in 1783; and for nearly thirty years its lectures were delivered in Cambridge, though its principal professors lived in Boston. In 1814 the Medical College in Boston was built, and at the same time the second story of Holden Chapel was arranged for an anatomical cabinet and lecture-room; costly anatomical preparations in wax, the best then attainable, were imported for use in the undergraduate department, and it was made the duty of the professor of anatomy to deliver annually a course of lectures to the senior class. Dr. John C. Warren had succeeded his father in the professorship, and had inherited and transcended his fame as a surgeon, — a fame transmitted unimpaired, as my readers well know, to his son and grandson. The elder Dr. Warren, as a popular lecturer, probably produced a more profound impression than his son; for there were still, when I was in college, echoes of the voice that had been silent for ten years or more, and there were resident graduates who used to say that they had never heard any thing so grand as the portions of his lectures that were not devoted to minute scientific detail, particularly those in which he illustrated the Divine wisdom and beneficence in the structure of the human frame. Yet, with these traditions, we found nothing wanting in the son. His lectures were as full as befitted their purpose, clear and explicit in statement, amply illustrated to the eye by a human skeleton and by life-like preparations of the interior organs, and by no means deficient in the eloquence of one who was the master equally of his subject and of his mother tongue. I had no subsequent acquaintance with Dr. Warren. I heard, indeed, much of his genius and skill, and of his personal peculiarities. I read and reviewed the elaborate memoir of him by his brother, my classmate and lifelong friend, Dr. Edward Warren. I hold his memory in honor and reverence for his preeminent services to his profession and to mankind, and for private virtues which could not remain hidden, though he took more pains to disguise them than to display them.

JOSEPH STORY.

(1798.)

I WAS brought up in the heart of Essex County Federalism; and it may illustrate the intenseness and stubbornness of political animosity in those times, when I say that all through my boyhood I heard Joseph Story's name as synonymous with all that is evil and hateful, on the sole ground of his activity as a leader of the Democratic party, though he had been appointed to the supreme bench of the United States during my birth-year, and had previously incurred the displeasure of the administration, and the strong resentment of Mr. Jefferson, by advocating in Congress the repeal of the embargo which at the outset had his warm support. Born in Marblehead, he practised law in Salem till he became judge; but the Salem Federalists hardly learned that he was a man to be proud of till he was ready to leave them, when they took their part in giving him a complimentary farewell dinner, and ever afterward deemed it an honor to the town to have had him for its citizen. It was greatly to the credit of Mr. Madison to have appointed Judge Story after he had broken fellowship with his party. I suppose that on the supreme bench there has not been his superior, unless it were Chief Justice Marshall; and it used to be said that he was of essential service to his chief's paramount reputation by his unsurpassed legal learning, which enabled him always to find precedents for the decisions which Judge Marshall was not unused to evolve from his own "inner consciousness." Dr. Dane, in establishing the professorship that bears his name, requested that Judge Story might be its first incumbent. In accordance with this wish and the concurrent desire of all the friends of the college, the appointment was made and accepted in 1829. At the same time, Mr. Ashmun was chosen Royall Professor of Law, with the understanding that he should have the immediate supervision of the Law School, while Judge Story was to devote to it such time as he could spare; and this was no little time, for he knew how to make his days elastic. There never was a man who did more work than he; and yet he knew not how to slight his work, or to put into it less of heart and soul than it could hold. With a body that seemed incapable of fatigue, he had the alertness and vivacity of youth, and imparted his own enthusiasm to his pupils.

I had repeated opportunities of profiting by his instruction. In the moot courts at which he presided in the Law School, he drafted juries among the divinity students; and I served several times in that capacity. He interested me so much on these occasions, that I once in a while strayed into his court in Boston, where, with perfect dignity, he maintained the same simplicity and ease as in the Dane Hall lecture-room. In the sessions of the Supreme Court in Washington, where the judges are ushered into the court-room with stately formalism, he probably wore a robe of the normal length; but in Boston his gown was a spencer, — a silk garment with ample sleeves, but without a skirt. His charges were perfect in point of explicitness, comprehensiveness, and adaptation to the non-legal mind; never deep, though the manifest result of deep thought; never technical, though on subjects that seemed to crave technical treatment; never dry or dull, though in cases that seemed wholly void of interest. I think that it could always be seen in what direction his own opinion turned; but he never failed to do full justice to both sides of the case in hand. His charges might have been too prolix for the eye, but not for the ear.

Judge Story, with fully two men's stated work, had time for every good cause and worthy enterprise. There was no public meeting for a needed charity, for educational interests, in behalf of art or letters, or for the advancement of a conservatively liberal theology, in which his advocacy was not an essential part of the programme. When there were no other speakers of note, it was enough to hear him; and he was not unwilling to occupy, and never failed to fill to the delight of his hearers, all the time that could be given him. When there were others whom it was desirable to hear, he was generally made chairman; and in his opening speech he always contrived to say as much as all those who followed him, and often unconsciously took the wind out of their sails. He formed a large part of the life of Cambridge society. His son is the only other man that I have ever known who could talk almost continuously for several successive hours, and leave his hearers with an appetite for more. Wherever Judge Story was, he did not usurp the conversation, but the floor was spontaneously and gladly conceded to him; and his listeners were entertained with an unintermitted flow of wit, humor, anecdote, literary criticism, comments on passing events, talk on the highest themes of thought, — the transition from topic to topic never abrupt, but always natural and graceful. He must have read by intuition; for he seemed to have read every thing, both old and new. I remember his admiration for Miss Austen's novels, which he regarded as superior to Scott's. In his youth he had published a volume of poems, the principal of which was on "The Power of Solitude," — a subject of which he must have been profoundly ignorant. In his latter years I know not whether he wrote poetry; but he talked it, and was familiar with the ephemeral poets of the day no less than with those who have their perennial place as classics.

Judge Story was a good citizen of Cambridge, and took an active part in all important municipal affairs. No man did more than he in securing for Cambridge the right to enclose the Common, in opposition to the towns lying farther in the interior, which claimed as of immemorial prescription the unrestricted and unbounded right of way for the herds of cattle that were driven through Cambridge to Brighton. In fine, one can hardly have filled a larger place in the community of his residence than he filled, with prompt and faithful service, with overflowing kindness and good will, and with the grateful recognition of people of every class and condition.

SIDNEY WILLARD.

(1798.)

HAD opportunity been commensurate with the power to render it availing, Professor Willard's name would be much better remembered than now, but not less reverently and lovingly by those who knew his worth. There are, to be sure, men who make opportunities; there are others who have them inevitably made, and unintentionally mis-made, for them, — for whom the ground on which they seem to have firm foot-hold is cut away from under their feet.

Sidney Willard studied theology after leaving college, and preached occasionally during the greater part of his life. His sermons were of exceptional merit in thought and style; and his faults of manner in his latter years were due, no doubt, to the infrequency of his appearance as a public speaker. He received, when a young man, at least two invitations to settle in the ministry, and was prevented from accepting them mainly by his reasonable expectation of permanent college employment. His father was president; and, though he carefully refrained from exercising any influence in his son's behalf, the teacher would have found full recognition. No man could have shown more patience than he manifested in the class-room: but nine-tenths of his pupils studied Hebrew solely because they were going to be ministers, and it was then discreditable to a minister to be utterly ignorant of Hebrew; while the general endeavor was to minimize the knowledge of it to the lowest degree. Mr. Willard wrote a Hebrew Grammar, which was adopted and used by Professor Stuart at Andover, and is immeasurably better for class-use than the cumbrous and clumsy grammar, anglicized and amplified from Gesenius, which Professor Stuart himself afterward published. Indeed, were Mr. Willard's grammar reprinted, with no essential changes or additions, and placed before the public with the prestige of newness, I think that any sensible teacher of Hebrew would regard it as a veritable godsend. But the proportion of grateful students — I will not say scholars — in the Hebrew tongue was, and I suppose still is, less than the one thankful leper bore to the ten that were cured.

At the time of Mr. Willard's appointment, John Quincy Adams accepted the Professorship of Rhetoric and Oratory, with the understanding that his sole duty should be the delivery of an annual course of lectures. The charge of the college themes was therefore committed to Mr. Willard, — a charge for which his excellent work as a critic in the early periodical literature to which I have alluded, and the rare endowments for such service manifested in

I loved the Hebrew language, and I owed my love for it to his fidelity and thoroughness as a teacher. He was a diffident man; and, knowing how little his students in general cared for Hebrew, he condoned their negligence, which must have been intensely annoying and painful to him. But there was no aid or facility which he did not rejoice to give to willing recipients of his kindness. He manifested in various ways his interest in the Divinity School. With the other professors, he attended the weekly preaching of the students, and gave, in his turn, his comments on the sermon, and on its mode of delivery, generally in two or three short, pithy, often epigrammatic sentences. In common with the other professors, he had his pseudonyme. He was called *Vâv*, from the Hebrew letter so named. *Yōd* is a curtailed *Vâv*, and, in its place in a word, is often "quiescent;" for such is the grammatical term. Mr. Willard used to bring his small boy to the evening preaching; and once, when the boy fell asleep, and lay on his father's knee, my next neighbor pointed to their seat, saying, "There's *Vâv* (ו), with *Yōd* (י) quiescent." The name *Yōd* thenceforth became attached to the boy.

After resigning his professorship, Mr. Willard, as sole editor, and, I suppose, sole proprietor, started "The American Monthly Review," which died at the end of two years, solely because it was too good to live. As I now look over the volumes, I regard the work as superior in merit to any literary review that has ever been published in this country. It was really a review; and its purpose was, without fear or favor, to tell the precise truth about new books or reprints as they appeared. The editor's own articles display great critical acumen and power of analysis. I find on the list of contributors a goodly array of the names then holding the highest place in science and literature, together with several young men, as Felton, Hillard, Peirce, Wendell Phillips, Sumner, who were already meriting the distinction that was early accorded to them. The younger members of the college Faculty were all Mr. Willard's personal friends, and eager to do their best in aid of his enterprise. Felton was foremost in his generous offices, as he always was whenever he could render service or kindness. In connection with this "Review," I recall the only instance in which, during an intimacy of between thirty and forty years, I ever saw Felton angry. He had written and sent to the press an article somewhat rhetorical, though by no means distastefully high-flown; and the proof came to him with "Froth" written in the margin against the most ambitious sentence in the copy. Felton went at once to the printer to complain of the insolence of his compositors in presuming to make insulting criticisms of the work under their hands. The explanation was promptly and satisfactorily given. At precisely that point, the work was passed over to a compositor named Frothingham.

The "Review" lost scores of subscribers on account of the two most able and learned articles that it contained. Professor Stuart, whose scholarship covered a vast area, but even in his own department had less depth than breadth, under the influence of some baleful star, prepared an edition of Cicero's "De Officiis," which was reviewed in "The American Monthly" with the most scathing and blighting criticism by Professor Kingsley of Yale College, then regarded as the first Latin scholar in America. Professor Stuart acknowledged the critic's justice and his own ill-advised temerity, and called in and burned all the unsold copies of his book. But, though Professor Kingsley was his co-religionist, the article was regarded as a sectarian assault on the most distinguished representative of the popular theology; and almost every Calvinistic subscriber withdrew his name.

About the same time, a certain D. J. Browne, who had obtained, I do not remember how, an extended popularity, published a treatise on geology, made up of bold thefts and atrocious blunders, which was reviewed with merited contempt by Dr. Samuel L. Dana, then the most eminent scientific man in this region. Mr. Browne had a very considerable clientage of sciolists, non-scientific admirers, and personal friends, who in large numbers withdrew their subscriptions from "The American Monthly." The list thus depleted was insufficient to authorize the continuance of the work, and was sold to "The New-England Magazine." Meanwhile the "Review" had attracted the most favorable notice in England; and, shortly after its discontinuance, there came to the publishers a larger English order than had ever been given for any American periodical.

Mr. Willard lived for twenty-three years after the termination of this enterprise. For a part of the time he was editor of "The Christian Register." He was often in the public service, for three years mayor of Cambridge, and several times a member of the House of Representatives and of the Executive Council. His life was one of unceasing industry and usefulness, and was enriched and adorned not only by the cardinal virtues, but equally by those delicate traits of peculiarly Christian excellence which make home happy, and win the affectionate regard of all within the sphere of their influence.

JOHN GORHAM.

(1801.)

Dr. Gorham was Adjunct Professor of Chemistry and Materia Medica from 1809 to 1816, and Professor of Chemistry and Mineralogy from 1816 to 1827. I never saw him. If my class can be said to have received any instruction in chemistry, other than from a few experiments, generally unsuccessful, it was from the then adjunct professor. Dr. Gorham held a high place in the public esteem as a physician, and used to be spoken of with admiration and affection.

BENJAMIN PEIRCE.

(1801.)

Mr. Peirce graduated at the head of his class, and was through his life a scholarly man, of refined literary taste, and with an easy and graceful style as a writer. I think that he never studied a profession. He entered into commerce in Salem, — his native town, — and maintained the highest character for probity, integrity, and honor. Reverses of fortune made him willing to resume a university life; and the Salem members of the corporation saw in him a man who could at once give academic dignity to the office of librarian, and bring to it the accurate business habits which the increase of the library demanded. In his official capacity he fully met their wishes, while he and his family formed a valuable and welcome addition to the academic society. He was appointed in 1826, and remained in office till his death in 1831. He left in manuscript a "History of Harvard University," which was prepared for publication by his fellow-townsman and lifelong friend, Hon. John Pickering, and published in 1833.

CHARLES SANDERS.

(1802.)

Mr. Sanders, another Salem man, brother-in-law of Mr. Peirce, was appointed steward on Mr. Higginson's resignation, with the view of establishing a rigid financial system in the details of college expenditure, similar to that initiated by Mr. Francis in the management of the funds. He came to Cambridge, not because he wanted the office, but because it was thought that the office wanted him. He was a rich man by the standard of the time; whether by inheritance, by the profits of business, or by both, I do not know. Generous and large-hearted in the use of his own funds, he practised in full the penny-wise, without being ever betrayed into the pound-foolish, policy, in behalf of the college. I doubt whether his accounts would show the expenditure of a single dollar which he could have saved. He held his office for four years, and remained a citizen of Cambridge till his death in 1864. He was a man of literary taste, of great practical wisdom, and of rare precision in manners and habits, living simply and inexpensively, but always ready with his tacit sympathy and liberal gifts, for any worthy cause, interest, or institution. Childless, he made the public his heir. Sanders Theatre represents his legacy to the college. He established by his will an agency for the promotion of temperance and kindred virtues,— in fine, a fund for the support of a lay missionary or minister at large, in Cambridgeport. He left the larger part of his property as a charity fund, the income to be expended at the discretion of trustees named in his will, with the power to appoint their successors. From the time that the income of this fund became availing, the trustees gave me annually, while I remained in office, from eight to twelve hundred dollars, for the benefit of such students in college as I found both needy and deserving; and since my resignation I think that they have still regarded Harvard students as holding a preferred place among their beneficiaries.

JOHN FARRAR.

(1803.)

MR. FARRAR became tutor in 1805, Professor of Mathematics and Natural Philosophy in 1807, and continued in the service of the college till, in 1836, he resigned his office, on account of incurable illness. His tutorship was in Greek; and he was educated for the ministry, — preached, I believe, a few times; but his professorship placed him where he belonged. I have no hesitation in saying that he was the most eloquent man to whom I ever listened. I doubt whether, after his early sermons, he was ever heard except in a college lecture-room; but he delivered, when I was in college, a lecture every week to the junior class on Natural Philosophy, and one to the senior class on Astronomy. His were the only exercises at which there was no need of a roll-call. No student was willingly absent. The professor had no notes, and commenced his lecture in a conversational tone and manner, very much as if he were explaining his subject to a single learner. But, whatever the subject, he very soon rose from prosaic details to general laws and principles, which he seemed ever to approach with blended enthusiasm and reverence, as if he were investigating and expounding divine mysteries. His face glowed with the inspiration of his theme. His voice, which was unmanageable as he grew warm, broke into a shrill falsetto; and with the first high treble notes the class began to listen with breathless stillness, so that a pin-fall could, I doubt not, have been heard through the room. This high key once reached, there was no return to the lower notes, nor any intermission in the outflow and the quickening rush of lofty thought and profound feeling, till the bell announced the close of the hour, and he piled up all the meaning that he could stow into a parting sentence, which was at once the climax of the lecture, and the climax of an ascending scale of vocal utterance, higher, I think, than is within the range of an ordinary soprano singer. I still remember portions of his lectures, and they now seem to me no less impressive than they did in my boyhood. I recall distinctly a lecture in which he exhibited, in its various aspects, the idea that in mathematical science, and in that alone, man sees things precisely as God sees them, — handles the very scale and compasses with which the Creator planned and built the universe; another, in which he represented the law of gravitation as coincident with, and demonstrative of, the divine omnipresence; another, in which he made us almost hear the music of the spheres, as he described the grand procession, in infinite space and in immeasurable orbits, of our own system and the (so-called) fixed stars. His lectures were poems, and hardly poems in prose; for his language was unconsciously rhythmical, and his utterances were like a temple chant. Nor have I ever seen or heard, even on the most sacred occasions, expressions of religious awe, adoration, faith, trust, and love, more fervent and inspiring, than from him in the class-room. I do not think that I am exaggerating. It was a time when there were not a few eloquent men within the hearing of Cambridge students, and we never lost an opportunity of hearing them. But, so far as I know, my coevals in college, such few of them as still survive, agree with me in giving the palm of eloquence to Professor Farrar.

I wish that he had left in print some fit memorial of his surpassing genius. But his pen was not idle. He published a series of twelve mathematical text-books; that is, on the several branches of pure and applied mathematics, including the various departments of physical science that demand mathematical treatment. These were, for the most part, translated and compiled from French treatises; but they were all prepared under his immediate oversight. They have been long since superseded, but I feel very sure that some of them have not been replaced.

Mr. Farrar was in private life genial and amiable, fond of society, and in conversation not unapt to grow eloquent on subjects worthy of his profound thought or feeling, and to show no little of the fervor of mien and utterance that gave such a charm defence of their authenticity and in exposition of their teachings. In early life he was a preacher; and those who in after-years hung upon his words, were always surprised to hear that he was unsuccessful in the pulpit. If this was the case, it must have been due to excess rather than to lack of merit, — to a preciseness of thought, statement, and utterance which, while surpassingly effective in the lecture-room, may have cramped his freedom of address to a promiscuous though intelligent audience. I deem it one of the great privileges of my life, that, during my first year in the Divinity School, I had his instruction in the exegesis of the New Testament. He united what might seem the opposite extremes of keen criticism and submissive faith. He carried to the investigation of the sacred writings the same microscopic scrutiny and uncompromising excision of whatever can be otherwise than genuine, which the great German scholars have brought to the study of the Greek and Roman classics. He was unwilling to take any thing for granted, — to believe any thing that he could not prove, or for which he had not the testimony of competent witnesses. In the Gospels he rejected every passage, every text, every word, in which he could discover any possible token of interpolation or of error in transcription; and the books thus expurgated he received, because he had convinced himself by research and reasoning that they were the veritable writings of the men whose names they bear, and the authentic record of Him whose life they portray. With this habit of mind, I do not by any means regard it as strange that his faith was intensely strong. I have never known a firmer belief than his in the divine mission and authority of Jesus Christ. Indeed, it seemed in him more than belief: it was knowledge. I doubt whether he felt any more confident assurance of the events daily occurring under his own eyes than of those which he supposed to have occurred within the cognizance of the apostles of Christ. The truths of the Christian revelation which transcend the sphere of human knowledge, he received implicitly, on the authority of him whom he believed to be an accredited teacher from God. In this faith he was serenely happy in his years of declining strength, and passed under the death-shadow with a hope based, not on his own speculations, but on what he regarded as the infallible testimony of One who knew.

It was impossible that such a man should not have approached and handled the sacred records with the profoundest reverence. Unsparing as he was in his criticism of their text, and in the rejection of much that was received by the Christian world in general, and even by Christian scholars, he always stood as with unshodden feet before what he recognized as the genuine word of God. I can still hear the echo of his intensely solemn intonations in repeating in his own version the Sermon on the Mount, or one of our Saviour's parables. He would rebuke, with a vehemence which recalled to our memory the traditions of the once strong but rigidly chastened passions of his earlier days, the student who made the slightest approach to flippancy with reference to the Scriptures or any of their contents. No man ever repeated the offence with him.

It may readily be supposed that Mr. Norton, while himself an arch-heretic in the eyes of (so-called) orthodox Christians, had little tolerance for what he deemed heresy. He was so sure of his own beliefs, that he could hardly imagine those who differed essentially from him to be both honest and wise. The transcendental school of thought, with its intuitive philosophy, found no sympathy from him. While no man felt more vividly than he, or expounded with greater fulness and beauty, the evidential value of Christ's character and teachings, he could not bear that the historical and external evidences of Christianity should be in any wise depreciated. He was equally hostile to rationalistic explanations of the supernatural narratives in the Gospels. He could get no satisfying glimpses of substantial truth in the cloudland in which the thinkers and students of Germany are wont to dwell, and he regarded even Goethe as having no rightful place in the hierarchy of really great minds.

In 1819 Mr. Norton commenced a work on the "Evidences of the Genuineness of the Gospels," the first volume of which appeared in 1837, the second and third in 1844. It constitutes an argument, the force of which has not been, and, as it seems to me, cannot be, invalidated. In the first volume, he concedes at the outset the postulates of those who claim for the Gospels an origin toward the middle of the second century, excludes all the earlier authorities, and throws over the chasm a bridge of circumstantial evidence, showing, and, as I think, demonstrating, that the unquestioned testimony of Irenæus and succeeding writers could not have been what it is, had not the Gospels been well known and fully accredited long before their time. He then quietly proceeds to fill in the chasm, and to supersede the bridge, by proving the validity of Justin Martyr and the earlier ecclesiastical writers as veritable witnesses to the genuineness, and no less to the authenticity, of the Gospels, though without specifying them by name. The second and third volumes are devoted to the incidental, yet, as the author thinks, and as I am inclined to think, conclusive, evidence of the genuineness of the Gospels furnished by the writings of the early heretics and the extant records of their beliefs. These volumes were followed by an elaborate criticism of Strauss's "Life of Jesus," and an unfinished work on the "Internal Evidence of the Genuineness of the Gospels," which were published in one volume after the author's decease. The "Translation of the Gospels," finished during his lifetime, was published after his death, with annotations, in part revised from his draft, and in part supplied by Ezra Abbot, who subsequently filled his professorship with like success and reputation.

Mr. Norton wrote a few poems of surpassing beauty. His poetry, like his prose, is characterized by a careful choice of words, a rare purity of diction, and a studied preciseness in the expression of thought, which, while never marring the rhythm, moderates the fire of his verse, and makes even his hymns meditative rather than lyrical, — yet meditative in the loftiest strain of devotion. Among these hymns are several which are to be found in many, and ought to be in all, hymnals, such as, —

> "My God, I thank thee! may no thought
> E'er deem thy chastisements severe!"

and

> "Oh, stay thy tears! for they are blest
> Whose days are past, whose toil is done," —

also, one less known, but of equal merit, —

> "Faint not, poor traveller, though thy way
> Be rough like that thy Saviour trod."

Among his pieces on subjects not conventionally sacred, though his Muse sanctified whatever it breathed upon, is the exquisite little poem entitled "Scene after a Summer Shower," commencing, —

> "The rain is o'er. How dense and bright
> Yon pearly clouds reposing lie!"

JACOB BIGELOW.

(1806.)

Dr. Bigelow, who was for forty years professor of Materia Medica, held from 1816 to 1827 the Rumford Professorship of the Application of Science to the Useful Arts. For the former of these professorships, he had very much the same qualification that a learned unbeliever might have for a professorship of Christian theology. No other man of his time had so little faith in drugs. Yet he was very learned in their historical and imagined uses, as is abundantly shown in his "Medical Botany." With this department, however, we collegians had no concern. His lectures as Rumford Professor were second only to Professor Farrar's in attractiveness; and, could the world have made no progress for sixty years, the full notes which we took of them — I have mine still — would be of inestimable value, and the two volumes of "Technology," in which he published their contents after his resignation, would not and could not have been superseded as a text-book. He gave us, with a well selected but meagre apparatus of models and diagrams, a wonderfully clear and vivid description of all the more important implements, processes, and products of the arts as they then were; but the chief use of his book now is as a waymark from which to measure the else incredible advance in every province of the industrial world. These lectures, in great part written, indicated in their style the high classical culture which, in his latter years, Dr. Bigelow was wont to depreciate. He lingered to a late old age, wise, genial, and kind, beloved and admired, with loss of sight, but with no failure in the keenness of his mental vision; and the only suggestion of second childhood that he gave his friends was his doubling upon his track as to the classic tongues, returning to the nursery, and making translations from Mother Goose into Greek lyrics of classic diction, faultless prosody, and melodious rhythm.

THOMAS NUTTALL.

(Hon. A. M. 1826.)

DRAKE, in his "Dictionary of American Biography," substituting what ought to have been for what was, says that Mr. Nuttall was Professor of Botany and Natural History from 1822 to 1834. In point of fact, on the death of Professor Peck, in 1822, the college found itself, and remained for twenty years, too poor to maintain a professorship in this department. Mr. Quincy, in his "History," says that Mr. Nuttall was appointed Curator of the Botanical Garden in 1822. In the Triennial Catalogue the appointment is said to have been made in 1825. His name was mythical to the members of college. We used to hear of him as the greatest of naturalists; but I never knew of his being seen. He lived in the house belonging to the Botanic Garden, in a then remote quarter of the town, which we seldom explored. I think that the catalogue promised in-of a reputation early won, and still earlier deserved, he was the first of the three men of cosmopolitan fame that have filled the Smith Professorship of the French and Spanish Literature and of Belles-Lettres, his only successors having been his friends, Longfellow and Lowell. There is no need of my giving a sketch of his life, for his Memoir has been generally read; and I must confine myself for the most part to personal reminiscences. I doubt whether he ever did any class-work: he certainly did not while I was in college. But he delivered, in alternate years, courses of lectures on French and on Spanish Literature, the last of these forming the substance of the first edition of his great work, the "History of Spanish Literature." These lectures had all the qualities of style and method which fitted them for an academic audience. We knew that they were of transcendent worth, and we listened to them eagerly and attentively. They were appreciated as highly, yet not so intelligently, as they would have been a few years later. They covered, for the most part, a then unknown territory. Spanish literature was known mainly by translations of the few world-famous authors; and, though the capacity of reading French was not rare, there were very few French books to be had, and those few, the works of the great writers of the seventeenth and eighteenth centuries, not the current literature of the time. But Mr. Ticknor did much toward awakening curiosity, and creating the condition of things in which he might have had an audience more fully conversant with the literatures of which he was master.

Mr. Ticknor deserves special commemoration for his services in the promotion of liberal culture and the advancement of knowledge. He was chief among the founders of the Boston Public Library. Still more, he was generous as to the use of his own library, which, in all departments stocked with the best authors in the best editions, was in his own department the richest and most valuable in the country. He never refused to lend a book, however precious; and his loans were so frequent as to require special registration as a guaranty against loss. I remember, that, when a young fellow-tutor of mine, not particularly intimate with him, wanted to write a lecture on the "Ireland Forgeries," Mr. Ticknor lent him the entire set of publications relating to them, probably the only set in the country, and consisting in part of *facsimiles* and privately printed monographs, which could not have been replaced. I knew not a few instances of similar kindness, indicating, no doubt, a broader charity than large pecuniary gifts would have implied.

WALTER CHANNING.
(1808.)

Dr. Walter Channing filled for about forty years an important professorship in the Medical School, and survived his graduation no less than sixty-eight years. He had no connection with the college proper; and I was acquainted with him only in the last years of his life, when I found him a charming *raconteur*, and knew him to be worthy of unqualified respect and reverence. He had, perhaps, more humor than fell to the lot of others of his distinguished family. It was related of him that on one occasion a gentleman having handed him a letter of introduction, he, on looking at the address, returned it, saying, "This is not for me, but for my brother William. The difference between us is, that he preaches, and I practise." Dr. Channing was the author of many treatises on specific subjects connected with his profession, as also of "Professional Reminiscences of Foreign Travel," and "A Physician's Vacation; or, a Summer in Europe," which last I remember having read with great pleasure.

EDWARD TYRREL CHANNING.

(Hon. A. M. 1819.)

PROFESSOR CHANNING entered college in 1804, and, as his biographer says, "was not graduated in course, as he was involved in the famous rebellion of 1807, one of the few in which the students seem, on the whole, not to have been in the wrong." I object to this statement as not broad enough. I am inclined to think that in college rebellions the students were always in the right as to principle, though injudicious in their modes of actualizing principle. There was not one of those rebellions in which the leaders were not among the foremost in their respective classes, in character no less than in scholarship. In the very last which occurred, more than half a century ago, a leader, if not pre-eminently the leader, was the first scholar of his class, and as truly a model of all Christian virtues then in his spotless youth, as when in his old age he closed a career second to none in honor and in usefulness, as a minister of the gospel. There were traditional maxims and methods of college jurisprudence to which the professorial mind had become hardened, which to unsophisticated youth justly seemed at variance with natural right; and there was no form of collective protest that they could make, which was not deemed rebellious in such a sense that they were compelled either to recant, or to leave college under censure. There were always some very excellent youth, who, generally under pressure from their parents, pursued the former course; but the latter was taken by a large proportion of those whom the college could least afford to lose. College rebellions have become impossible, because the rights of the students are now fully recognized, their sense of honor held sacred, their protests and complaints considered carefully and kindly, and their unintended wrongs relieved and remedied, even though it involve the admission of mistake, or error of judgment, on the part of the Faculty, which in earlier times would have been regarded as subversive of discipline and authority.

Mr. Channing, on leaving college, commenced the

study of law with his elder brother, Francis, and was in due time admitted to the bar. Whether he succeeded, or aimed at success, as a lawyer, probably no one now among the living knows. It is known, however, that he was not only a diligent, but a deep, student, and that the expectation of his friends was that he would become a distinctively learned and philosophical jurist. He bore part in the essays at a higher periodical literature which issued in the establishment of "The North American Review," of which he was the editor for a year, resigning the charge on his election to the Professorship of Rhetoric and Oratory, in 1819, in the twenty-ninth year of his age.

This appointment was perhaps the most important ever made in the interest of American literature. The requirements of the college were then, happily, such as to afford the largest scope for the professor's work; and the classes were so small that he could individualize his instruction as it would be impossible to do now that a single class outnumbers any four, or certainly any three, that ever came under his hands. The students then were obliged to write themes once a fortnight for the whole of the last three years. These themes were written on the old-fashioned broad letter-sheet, with a wide margin for criticism. The professor had a system of notation, designating by letters or arbitrary signs all conceivable omissions, faults, or errors, whether in orthography, syntax, rhetoric, or reasoning, with parallels (‖)

to indicate faultlessness, either of the whole theme or of a single paragraph. As may well be supposed, *unparalleled* merit was the common lot: the exceptions were regarded as of much greater worth than high marks or tokens of success in any other department. On a specified day, Mr. Channing remained in session for several consecutive hours, received the members of the class one by one, and, guided by his own marks in the margin, made a minute criticism of the theme, not sparing censure for carelessness, or ridicule for whatever was pretentious, pompous, inflated, or otherwise than natural. If there was a single word that did not contribute to the meaning of the sentence, it was marked for excision. Exaggerations of all kinds were toned down. The student was shown how to say precisely what he meant, and nothing more. Superfluous epithets and mixed metaphors were dealt with unmercifully. Meanwhile euphony was not neglected; and we were taught that sound, while kept subordinate to sense, is never undesirable as its auxiliary. Thus, a jejune style was trained into roundness and melody, while ambitious diction of every sort was made to have a hollow ring. There were errors and deformities of style that were so dealt with that it was hardly possible that Mr. Channing's pupil should be guilty of them more than once; for his invectives against them were so keenly pointed as to inhere lastingly in any mind capable of comprehending them. So manifest was his influence, that, when more mob, and whose "shade" Washington came from the land of shadows to "receive," — a passage which I can still repeat, and which transcends in bombast all else that I have ever read or heard or imagined. Mr. Channing listened attentively to these declamations, and marked them, I think, on a scale of twenty-four; but he never made any comment, unless it were to rebuke the choice of a piece offensively coarse, or some outrageous grotesqueness in delivery.

Professor Channing read annually a course of lectures, which — published after his death — are models of rhetorical finish, and full of valuable thought, precept, and criticism, but which were delivered in so slovenly a way as to attract very little attention, and to perform but a scanty portion of the service which they were fitted to render.

In social life Mr. Channing was justly a favorite. He was a much better talker than his more eminent brother, the divine of world-wide celebrity, whose tendency in conversation was to monologue, often grand, sometimes prosy and repetitious. Among those on his own plane of high culture, Professor Channing never held a second place; while in the ordinary intercourse of society he so blended wit and wisdom, that no man could make himself more entertaining, or to better purpose. At the same time, he was genial in his relations with the students, conspicuously kind in every thing save his treatment of their themes, and substantially so, to their enduring gratitude, in his severest strictures and most stinging sarcasms, which were never without justifying cause.

JONATHAN BARBER.

The first professedly scientific teacher of elocution employed in Harvard College was Dr. Barber, an English physician, who also taught elocution in Yale College, and was at a subsequent period professor of oratory in McGill University at Montreal. I am inclined to think that he was an accomplished trainer of the vocal organs; and in that respect his system and method very closely resembled those of that well-remembered and justly revered teacher, William Russell. He was also a man of respectable character, zealous in his work, and disposed to hold pleasant relations with his pupils. But he was pompous and fantastic in mien, speech, and manners. Then, too, oratory was with him a mere mechanical art, not a power of soul with the voice for its instrument. His great glory was the invention, unique, I suppose, of a hollow sphere, six feet in diameter, made of some six or eight bamboo rods, which were its meridians, and were crossed by an equator, by at least two great circles besides, and by an adequate number of small circles corresponding to parallels of latitude. In this sphere the student stood to declaim, and the circles by their various altitudes and intersections determined the gestures appropriate to each specific mood of feeling, or form of mental action.

Not being then a member of college, I was outside of Dr. Barber's *sphere*. But those who were in it had a great deal of fun in it, and got a great deal of fun out of it, — so much, that, when it was discovered one morning ignominiously suspended on a *barber's* pole opposite the college yard, it was withdrawn from use.

Dr. Barber had in his family a step-son, and prospective son-in-law, who had been educated in England, was a classical scholar of large attainments and exquisite taste, and has been for many years one of the most learned and eminent jurists in British North America. This young man was made tutor, and, while "apt to teach," betrayed his juvenility and inexperience in various ways that brought him into unpleasant collision with the students. As it was then the traditional maxim that a college officer, right or wrong, should always be sustained by the Faculty, his tutorship had its not unnatural issue in the last great college rebellion. His connection with the college terminated at or before the close of the year of his appointment (1834–35); and his step-father at the same time suspended college work for a season, to become a lecturer on phrenology.

EDWARD EVERETT.

(1811.)

The public yet awaits, with an impatience diminishing as the years roll on, the memoir of Mr. Everett, which his son undoubtedly will furnish, it is to be hoped before the desire for it dies away. My purpose is to give merely my own personal reminiscences. I first heard Mr. Everett, without seeing him, in 1819, at the funeral of Rev. Dr. Bentley of Salem. I was a small boy, but already a good listener. I was taken to the church in which the funeral was held, and was seated in a high gallery-pew, over which I could not obtain so much as a single glimpse of the officiating clergy. Mr. Everett had withdrawn from the pulpit; but Dr. Bentley was expected to leave his very valuable library to Harvard College;[1] and, in honor of its supposed benefactor, the clerical force of the college took the main charge of the funeral, and Mr. Everett resumed his clerical function to preach the sermon, probably his last. I well remember the silver[2] tones of his voice,

[1] The college gave Dr. Bentley the degree of Doctor of Divinity at the Commencement before his death; but it had been anticipated by Alleghany College, which then was a mere name, yet had, by its power of conferring degrees, secured the bequest of several valuable libraries, Dr. Bentley's among the rest. Dr. Bentley's probably contained a larger number of rare books and editions than any other private library in New England. Alleghany College, at Meadville, Penn., is now, under Methodist auspices, a flourishing institution: but in 1828, as I personally know, and for several years later, the college was four brick walls, unfinished and roofless; and the library, almost utterly useless, was kept by sufferance in a small apartment in the court-house.

[2] I use the term *silver*, not as the hackneyed term which it has become, as applied to any voice that has the element of sweetness. The *timbre* of Mr. Everett's voice resembled very closely that of the bells which have in their metal the largest proportion of silver. Several years ago, in listening to the bells of Moscow, which have a *maximum* of silver, and are kept ringing a large part of the time, I was perpetually reminded of Mr. Everett's oratory.

and can recollect portions of his sermon. It was, though not a vision, an early experience, of rare eloquence.

I first saw Mr. Everett when I was examined for admission to college in 1823. The candidates for admission were then divided into thirteen sections, corresponding to the thirteen apartments in University Hall (including the chapel and dining-rooms) that could be brought into use for the examination. The examination began at six o'clock in the morning, and, with a half-hour's intermission for dinner, lasted till sunset. Each of thirteen college officers took a section, and passed it over to the next, and so on, until it had gone the entire round. It was my good fortune, with three or four other timid boys, to begin with Mr. Everett, who examined us in Greek poetry. He received us so kindly, gave us such an encouraging view of the ordeal before us, and dismissed us with such well-framed advice as to the self-possession and quietness of spirit requisite for our success, that I have always ascribed my entrance without condition in great part to my having started for the day's work under his auspices.

I next saw and heard him in his Phi Beta Kappa oration in 1824, when he made that memorable address of welcome to Lafayette. It was undoubtedly the greatest moment of his life as an orator. No description can do justice to the scene, or to its effect on the audience. It was the perfection of art, with every grace that belongs to nature. Had the occasion been sprung upon him without a moment's warning, his utterance could not have seemed more spontaneous; while there was the exquisite completeness of diction, voice, and gesture, to which the most elaborate preparation could have added nothing.

Though Mr. Everett did not formally resign his professorship till 1826, he performed no college duty, and, I think, did not even live in Cambridge, after I entered college in 1824. He lived for several years in Charlestown, and I remember having been at a party in his house there in 1833. I was not, however, an habitual visitor at his house, and saw him but seldom; yet on several occasions I received very great kindness from him. He aided me in my researches in my then favorite department of political economy, by sending me public documents. I was indebted to him repeatedly for advice and furtherance in my editorship of "The North American Review," and at my request he wrote an article for me.

I heard his famous lecture on Washington three times; and in connection with its delivery I chanced to see more of him, and more intimately, than at any other period. That lecture was the most marvellous master-work of rhetorical art and skill of which I have ever had any knowledge. Washington's character, in its massive simplicity and perfectness, afforded very little hold for popular eloquence. Mr. Everett, fully aware of this, grouped around the honored name a vast number and an immense diversity of men, incidents, objects of admiration in nature and curiosity in art, scientific facts, classical allusions, myths of the gods of Greece, — the greater part of them not in themselves illustrative of his theme, but all of them pressed into its service, and forced into an adaptation that was made at the time to appear natural and obvious. A catalogue of the materials used in that lecture would seem as heterogeneous as the contents of a country variety shop, and a man of ordinary genius would have won only ridicule in the attempt to bring them together. But Mr. Everett compressed them into perfect and amazing unity, and rendered them all subsidiary to the praise and fame of Washington; while, when the lecture was over, it was impossible to recollect what bearing on the character of our first President was assigned to the greater part of them. I first heard the lecture in Boston. A few weeks afterward he delivered it in Portsmouth, N.H., where I then lived, and shared with the friend at whose house he staid the charge and pleasure of his hospitable reception. We took him to the family mansion where Tobias Lear, Washington's private secretary, was born, and where Washington, on his Northern tour during his presidency, was a guest, and introduced him there to an old lady, Mr. Lear's niece, who had in her parlor the very sofa on which Washington had sat, holding her on his knee, and a sampler which she had wrought with a long lock of his white hair which he gave her. Mr. Everett, without seeking time for special preparation, so worked the Lear house, its occupant, and its furniture, into the appropriate part of his lecture, that the whole story seemed absolutely inseparable from what preceded and what followed, and as if it had been written in its place in the beginning. A short time afterward I went to Brunswick to deliver the Phi Beta Kappa address, and he was going to deliver his Washington lecture in the evening. I was his fellow-guest at the house of his cousin, Hon. Ebenezer Everett. It was incidentally said at table that "all Bath" was coming up to hear him, arrangements having been made for a special train. A short time previously the wife of a Bath ship-master, disabled by paralysis, — though herself in a condition that might have excused her from active duty, — had taken command of her husband's ship, in the harbor of San Francisco, and brought it home in good order to Bath. That story Mr. Everett incorporated into his lecture, entering with the utmost delicacy into the circumstances that rendered the achievement the more heroic and noteworthy; and there was no portion of the lecture which seemed more closely adapted to the subject, or which the hearers would have missed more had they heard the discourse again elsewhere. Yet, when Mr. Everett had gone to his room, we found it impossible to recall the process by which he had dovetailed this story into his lecture, or the precise bearing which it had on the merit and fame of Washington.

duty so enfeebled him that he never recovered sound health or full working power. During his absence in Europe, and while he was supposed to be rapidly convalescent, a Professorship of Pulpit Eloquence and Pastoral Care was established in connection with the Divinity School, with the view of securing his services, the worth of which his pupils cannot overestimate. His, indeed, was the work of an invalid, yet performed with such practical wisdom, such intensity of devotional feeling, such delicate sense of the capacities, needs, and sensibilities of individual students, and such intimacy of friendly relation with them, that they sustained no loss by infirmities which made his life a constant weariness, and brought it to its close in what would else have been its meridian. His appointment bears even date with my entering the Divinity School. I do not remember that he read to us any lectures; but he met us once or twice a week, sometimes for a talk on pastoral duty, sometimes for instruction in sermon-writing, or for an exposition of the importance, due place, and fit methods of *extempore* preaching, and then, again, for the reading and discussion of our skeletons of sermons on previously assigned texts or subjects. On these occasions, though there was no digression from the subject in hand, there was an undercurrent of profound religious emotion, which was continually rising to the surface, and brimming over, so as to make the lecture-room a sanctuary. He at the same time gave to our fledgeling sermons the most faithful, thorough, and judicious criticism. The senior and middle classes preached, each member in his turn, on Friday and Saturday evenings. Mr. Ware took our sermons home, and invited the preacher to breakfast on some specified morning shortly afterward. We had thus the privilege of participating in his family worship, — always both edifying and instructive, — and a half-hour with his lovely wife, whose rich endowments of mind were hardly transcended by her unsurpassed beauty of character, and her lifelong, in some instances grandly heroic, philanthropy. From the table we went into the professor's study, where our sermons were literally taken to pieces and reconstructed. Long introductions, feeble and dragging perorations, obscurity of statement, breaks in the progress of thought, violations of good taste, florid rhetoric, — all were kindly, but unsparingly, pointed out and commented on; while the tone of his strictures was such as to make us feel how much more of genuine Christian instruction and edification the subject and plan might have been made to yield than we had embodied in the manuscript in hand. The result often was a voluntary re-writing of the sermon for his inspection and approval; while such volunteer sermons as we submitted to him always received his most careful examination, and his impartial estimate of their merits and their deficiencies.

We had, also, a great deal of informal intercourse

with Mr. Ware. He sometimes called on us at our rooms; we were always welcome, and often invited visitors, at his house: and I know not how adequately to express my sense of the educational value of a three-years' intimacy with such a man, in preparation for the Christian ministry.

Mr. Ware's influence was largely felt, too, in the college. He became the Sunday-morning preacher, and no one could have been better fitted for an academic audience. His sermons were of sufficiently strong intellectual staple to win respect for his ability as a thinker and a writer; while they were replete with devotional sentiment, and so delivered as to make them seem like spontaneous utterances from heart to heart. Had his health permitted, he would undoubtedly have devised modes of meeting more directly the religious needs of the undergraduates. As it was, many of them sought his acquaintance, and came under his influence; and several of our most able ministers looked to him as their spiritual father, and ascribed the choice of their profession, and the heart with which they entered it, to their intercourse with him.

CHARLES FOLSOM.

(1813.)

It is hard to say why Mr. Folsom did not fill as conspicuous a place, as he left a distinguished reputation, in the world of letters. There were not a few for whom he contributed very largely to a fame which it might have seemed easy for him to share or to surpass. At different times, tutor, instructor in Italian, and librarian in Harvard College, he resigned the latter office in 1826, and then, or shortly afterward, became connected with the University Press, and, for a time at least, a partner in the business. His department here was that of a proof-reader; and he made this department again what it was in the days when it was in the hands of Grotius and his peers in scholarship, a truly liberal profession. An author who passed through his hands sometimes would hardly recognize his own work in its improved dress. Mr. Folsom's only error was in the excess of thoroughness. He would consult scores of authorities on the use of a particle; and there was current a myth, not without verisimilitude, that he at one time kept the press idle for several days because he could not satisfy himself whether a comma should be retained, or a semicolon substituted. He was obliged, by the slowness of his painstaking accuracy, to resign the charge of the proofs in the preparation of Worcester's English Dictionary; but were there ten or twelve men like him, who could divide between them the superintendence of a similar work, we might have a dictionary free from such deficiencies and blunders as in several instances have been blindly copied by a series of successive lexicographers, and still disfigure some of the latest and most pretentious works of that kind.

I do not know that Mr. Folsom ever appeared before the public as an author, though he must undoubtedly have contributed to the periodical literature of his time. The only specimen of his capacity as a writer, to which I have access, is a letter on the care and use of public libraries, which can hardly be transcended in simplicity, purity, and elegance of diction. His skill as an editor was manifested in the "Select Journal of Foreign Periodical Literature," which he published in 1833 and 1834, in connection with Professor Norton, whose other pursuits made it necessary for Mr. Folsom to assume by far the larger part of the labor and responsibility. This work was the earliest of its kind, and, it seems to me, the best. Its four volumes on my shelves are the richest collection of literary miscellanies within my knowledge, and contain many articles which are as well worth reading now, after the interval of more than half a century, as they were interesting on their first appearance. Indeed, it would seem as if the selection were made with prime reference to the intrinsic and enduring merit of the several articles.

Mr. Folsom's ability as an accomplished classical scholar was evinced in two works prepared for school and college use, which held a foremost place for a long series of years, — a selection of Cicero's Orations, and a selection from Livy, both with English notes that could not have been better adapted to their purpose.

After closing his connection with the University

Press, Mr. Folsom held the office of librarian of the Boston Athenæum for eleven years. The last sixteen years of his life were a period of literary leisure and enjoyment, among Cambridge friends who were instructed and enriched by his conversation, and whom he was always happy to aid in their researches, and to serve by his keen, unerring, and kindly criticism. He was to the last a busy man; but the fruits of his industry were for the most harvested by those whose only return could be their thanks and their grateful remembrance. He died in 1872.

To what of Mr. Folsom's career came within my personal knowledge, I cannot forbear adding an episode of his early life, in which he was very near becoming both more and less of a man than he actually was,—more in the eyes of the larger public; less in the cherished memory of the few who enjoyed his intimacy. From 1816 to 1821 he was, first, chaplain and teacher of mathematics on board the seventy-four gun-ship "Washington;" then, *chargé d'affaires* of the United States at Tunis; then, secretary of Commodore Bainbridge, on a diplomatic mission to Turkey. In these several offices he displayed the ability and diligence which in those better days would have insured his continuance and promotion in the public service, but for his preference of literary labor. Among his pupils on board the "Washington" was Midshipman, afterward Admiral, Farragut, who always spoke of him with admiration and gratitude, and, on his visit to Boston after the close of the civil war, presented him with a magnificent silver vase, with inscriptions commemorative of their joint life in the Mediterranean.

JOHN WARE.

(1813.)

Dr. Ware was the second son of Rev. Dr. Henry Ware, senior, and probably resembled his father more nearly than any other member of the numerous family. He was for many years in the full practice of the medical profession in Boston. For a few years he had his home in Cambridge; but it was during a period when I had no immediate connection with the college, and my personal knowledge of him was very slight. He was a professor in the Medical School for more than a quarter of a century, and, equally as a teacher and as a physician, was regarded as pre-eminently wise. A man who holds a very high place among the elder members of the medical profession told me, not long ago, that he had never known a physician whose judgment in the diagnosis, and discretion in the treatment, of disease seemed to him equal to Dr. Ware's. At the same time, he possessed the traits of moral excellence which belonged by hereditary right to his father's children.

THADDEUS WILLIAM HARRIS.

(1815.)

Dr. Harris, who for twenty-five years was librarian of Harvard College, was second to no naturalist of his time in his scientific attainments in the department of natural history (as it was then called), and won special eminence by two great works on entomology, which have lost none of their value in the progress of the science to which they belong. He contributed largely to various periodicals, and to the "Encyclopædia Americana." Though he does not appear in the Triennial Catalogue as a professor or instructor, he had at times classes of college students in natural history, and founded among his pupils a permanent society for its study. He was a retiring, modest man, who rather evaded than sought the distinction and honor that were his of right; and his high and enduring reputation rested wholly on his merits, and not on his claims. In private and domestic life he was worthily beloved; and those of his associates in the college Faculty who enjoyed his intimacy held him in the dearest regard as a man equally of rare intellectual endowments, and of the most estimable character.

GEORGE OTIS.

(1815.)

George Otis, as tutor, was at the head of the Latin department, and for most of the time the only Latin instructor, from 1820 to 1826, when he was made professor in accordance with a statute of the University then existing, which provided that tutors at the end of six years of acceptable service should become professors. In the general retrenchment, brought about by the Salem administration, Mr. Otis was asked to resign in 1827; and the department remained for five years without a professor.

Mr. Otis was an accomplished scholar, an admirable teacher, of superior general culture, of refined tastes, and of manners at once dignified, courteous, and kind. In the class-room he conformed to the general habit of simply hearing the students recite, without any express oral instruction; but he contrived so to manage his recitations as to test the scholarship of his pupils, and to bring out, either through them or in supplementing their deficiencies, the points in the successive lessons that claimed special attention. At the same time he was ready to receive at his room such students as desired to read Latin out of course, and he made those private exercises equally pleasant and profitable. In company with a classmate I thus read with him a part of Lucan's "Pharsalia," and have retained the most grateful remembrance of his instruction, and of my intercourse with him.

the class — often made too large even by good men — of acts morally indifferent, and carried the question of right or wrong into the smallest details of daily life, recognizing no distinction between greater and lesser duties. Faithfulness, thoroughness, and indefatigable industry characterized his entire life-work.

His father's misfortunes in business left him early dependent on his own exertions and merits. Working his way to a foremost reputation as a young scholar and preacher, at the age of twenty-two he became pastor of the church in Brattle Square, Boston, where, as the successor of Thacher, Buckminster, and Everett, he more than filled their place, not, indeed, by the eloquence which had made that pulpit illustrious, but by sermons that were master-works of patient, profound, and clear thought, pervaded, too, by devout sentiment too deep to seem emotional, yet so genuine as always to be recognized and felt as the motive-power of his preaching. At the same time, he was unremittingly assiduous in his parochial service, and took special charge of the religious training of the children and youth under his pastorate, laying out for them a systematic course of scriptural and ethical instruction, extended through a series of years, and adapted to render them much more than sciolists in sacred things. Unwilling to occupy as a teacher ground on which he was not a constant learner, he was earnest and enterprising in the critical study of the Scriptures, conversant with the best literature in that department, and one utmost kindness, and commended to the careful consideration of the class, my somewhat elaborate statement of a widely different exegesis, which I had written out at his request, and in which I still think that I was in the right. During his tenure of office, Dr. Palfrey preached in the college chapel several series of sermons of surpassing merit, specially adapted to the needs of a university congregation. I doubt whether any preacher was ever listened to more intently or with a more serious interest than he was in that pulpit. I remember particularly a series of ethical sermons, methodical in arrangement, exhaustive in division, philosophically sound, and religiously impressive, based on the intrinsic and eternal Right, at the same time intensely emphatic in the recognition of the one Teacher of morals who could speak with divine authority, and appealing constantly to his example of pure and holy living. Dr. Palfrey's style of composition for the pulpit was unique, and I have always ascribed its peculiarities to his minute and painstaking truthfulness. Afraid of overstatement, he inserted in a single sentence all needed qualifications, exceptions, and explanations; so that the sentence might stand by itself as representing precisely what he meant to convey, neither more nor less. His sentences were, therefore, packed so full of meaning as to seem to the eye involved and obscure. But not so to the ear. He had what I might call a pictorial mode of utterance, — a vocal *chiaro-oscuro*, — so that it was easy to give its due light or shadow to each general statement, to every modifying clause, and to parenthesis within parenthesis, even to the third degree. His delivery was animated without being impassioned; and to the hearer perspicuity, equally with precision, characterized his discourses. In later years, especially in historical writing, his style became to the eye what it always was to the ear. Facts did not need the careful qualifying which abstract thought required.

In addition to his other labors, Dr. Palfrey assumed the editorship of "The North American Review," and conducted it successfully for ten years. After resigning his professorship in 1839, he delivered two courses of lectures before the Lowell Institute on subjects connected with the evidences of Christianity, both of which were published. He also published in four octavo volumes his "Lectures on the Jewish Scriptures and Antiquities" delivered before the Divinity School. This work gives evidence of profound study, earnest research, vigorous thought, and a teaching power seldom equalled. It maintains theories with regard to the Old Testament coincident or parallel with those then generally received among Christian scholars, which, so far as they have ceased to be maintained, have been dropped rather for lack of evidence as to writings of so obscure antiquity than for proof to the contrary, and which have no better exposition or more able advocacy than can be found in these volumes.

While employed in his editorial charge, and engaged in writing his Lowell lectures, Dr. Palfrey declined preaching, on the ground that he had no time to prepare new sermons, and that he could not conscientiously give to Christian congregations the fruit of less mature years, while he was conscious of a growing capacity for intellectual labor. He did not mean to withdraw permanently from the pulpit: in fact, he never re-entered it. He, of course, did not actively seek employment as a preacher; and it seems to have been tacitly taken for granted that he had deserted the profession which had, on the other hand, deserted him. Had he proclaimed his readiness to resume his place as a preacher, there were many churches where his services would have been warmly welcomed; but it may be that in the pulpits where his re-appearance would else have been most eagerly sought, his clearly avowed anti-slavery sentiments might have interfered with his cordial acceptance. That he did not return to the pulpit, was his lifelong regret. Meanwhile he drifted into political life, and was successively a member of the Massachusetts Legislature, Secretary of the State of Massachusetts, and Representative in Congress, — also, for six years postmaster of Boston.

In 1844 occurred a most memorable episode in Dr. Palfrey's life. His father had taken to Louisiana the remnants of his once considerable property, had invested them in newly settled lands of increasing value on Red River, and had become possessed of what grew to be a valuable plantation, with its necessary appendage of a large family of slaves. On his father's death, John claimed his full heritage of the "souls of men," no less than of lands and goods. He went to New Orleans to enforce his claim. I was there at that time, and became acquainted with details, which, in his modesty, he was at no pains to make public. His fellow-heirs urgently offered to pay him his share of the property in money, and to keep possession of the slaves. When he declined this proposal, legal impediments were thrown in his way; and the affair became a subject of popular excitement, which would have seemed ominous of peril to a man less resolute in the right. But, deeming it a matter of imperative duty, he held his ground, and received at length his full share of the human property. He was suffered to choose his portion, and he chose those to whom slavery seemed the most fully fraught with evil and peril. One negro in particular, who had waited upon him, and become attached to him, and whom he would have been glad to have as a servant, earnestly begged for this privilege; but it was denied on the ground that he was too valuable to be otherwise than prized and well cared for in his bondage. Dr. Palfrey's freed men and women he, of course, brought to the North at his own charge, maintained his guardianship over them till they were capable of self-support, kept up his correspondence with them for years afterward, and took pleasure in showing daguerreotypes of some of them. They cost him more than all the residue of his patrimony.

Sent to Congress by the Free-soil party in 1847, he was dropped by them at the next election, because he was not sufficiently pronounced in his anti-slavery utterances; that is, because he preferred acting the right to denouncing the wrong.

The principal literary labor of Dr. Palfrey's later years was his "History of New England." This has the prime merit of authenticity. He spared no labor to secure accuracy, even in the minutest details. He made several visits to England for the examination of public documents. He visited in various parts of New England the scenes of important events,[1] gathered and sifted local traditions, and sought out whatever matter in print or in manuscript could furnish contemporary records of men and all their doings. His style as an historian is clear, pure, graphic, and vigorous, rigidly precise in statement, often pictorial, and especially remarkable for lifelike descriptions of character. There are some sketches of well-known personages that are almost unequalled in their kind for raciness, pith, and point, and are possessed of a literary merit even transcending their historical value. Take, for instance, his summary of

[1] One such visit came very near issuing in one of the few, if any, of the inaccuracies in detail to be found in his History. In order to furnish a strictly circumstantial narrative of an Indian raid and massacre of no little historical importance, he took notes on the spot, and, in accordance with them, described the residence of one of the victims as on the margin of a beautiful lake. Reading the sketch to the friend whose guest he had been on this visit, he was informed that the pond, though fed by living springs, and looking as if it had always been there, owed its origin to the enterprise of his host.

Governor Stoughton's life-record, too long to quote entire, closing with the sentence, "He meant to be excellently firm: he excelled in being churlish, morose, and obstinate, in a style of the most unimpeachable dignity."

Dr. Palfrey's power of continuous literary labor outlasted his fourth score of years. For three or four years longer he lingered under growing infirmity and with much suffering, but with mental faculties unimpaired, and a patience, serenity, and repose of Christian faith and hope over which passed not a momentary cloud. He asked that the hymn,

"There is a land of pure delight,"

might form a part of his funeral service; and his life for many months had seemed consciously on the confines of that land, its dawning sunlight illumining the shadow of death, as it quietly crept, and slowly closed, over his earthly vision.

PIETRO BACHI.

(Hon. A. M. 1827.)

Dr. Bachi was educated at the University of Padua, where he received the degree of J.U.D. He was a lawyer by profession. Implicated in the political troubles of 1815, he was banished, and lived in England till 1825, when he came to this country, and was for twenty years teacher of Italian and Portuguese in Harvard College. He published an Italian Grammar, which had great reputation in its time. He was a man of learning, of fine appearance, and of gentlemanly manners, and had entire success as an instructor until, not without reason, he forfeited the respect and confidence of his associates and pupils.

CHARLES FOLLEN.

Dr. Follen received his degree in arts, and his doctorate of the civil law, from the University of Giessen, where he also lectured on various branches of jurisprudence. At an early stage of his career, having been disposed to regard all religions as equally worthless, he was led to make a thorough investigation of the claims of Christianity. The result was a firm and devout Christian faith; and, in connection with this epoch of his life, he gave as his own experience what, I am disposed to believe, represents the consciousness of many other inquirers: "I can certainly say, that, next to the Gospel itself, the books that have been written against it have been the most efficient promoters of my belief in its divine truth." Persecuted and virtually exiled from Germany, on political grounds, he sought refuge in Switzerland, where he filled important educational places, especially in the University of Basle. Finding himself liable to extradition at the demand of the German Government, he took passage for America, landed in New York, and through the influence of Messrs. Du Ponceau and Ticknor, whom Lafayette, then in this country, had interested in his behalf, received, in 1825, an appointment as instructor in German in Harvard College. German had never been taught in college before; and it was with no little difficulty that a volunteer class of eight[1] was found, desirous, or at least willing, to avail themselves of his services. I was one of that class. We were looked upon with very much the amazement with which a class in some obscure tribal dialect of the remotest Orient would be now regarded. We knew of but two or three persons in New England who could read German; though there were probably many more, of whom we did not know. There were no German books in the bookstores. A friend gave me a copy of Schiller's "Wallenstein," which I read as soon as I was able to do so, and then passed it from hand to hand among those who could obtain nothing else to read. There was no attainable class-book that could be used as a "Reader." A few copies of Noehden's Grammar were imported, and a few copies of I forget whose "Pocket Dictionary," fortunately too copious for an Anglo-Saxon pocket, and suggesting the generous amplitude of the Low Dutch costume, as described in Irving's mythical "History of New York." The "German Reader for Beginners," compiled by our teacher, was furnished to the class in single sheets as it was needed, and was printed in Roman type, there being no

[1] In one of his letters he speaks of having, at this time, thirty pupils. He very probably had a class in Boston. I think that I cannot be mistaken as to the number of his first college class.

German type within easy reach.[1] There could not have been a happier introduction to German literature than this little volume. It contained choice extracts in prose, all from writers that still hold an unchallenged place in the hierarchy of genius, and poems from Schiller, Goethe, Herder, and several other poets of kindred, if inferior, fame. But in the entire volume, Dr. Follen rejoiced especially in several battle-pieces from Körner, the soldier and martyr of liberty, whom we then supposed to have been our teacher's fellow-soldier, though, in fact, he fell in battle when Dr. Follen was just entering the University. I never have heard recitations which impressed me so strongly as the reading of those pieces by Dr. Follen, who would put into them all of the heart and soul that had made him too much a lover of his country to be suffered to dwell in it. He appended to the other poems in the first edition of the Reader, anonymously, a death-song in memory of Körner, which we all knew to be his own, and which we read so often and so feelingly, that it sank indelibly into permanent memory; and I find that after an interval of sixty years it is as fresh in my recollection as the hymns that I learned in my childhood. This song I am sure will be gladly read again by any of Dr. Follen's early pupils who may be still living, and I quote it entire. I have endeavored in vain to satisfy myself with a translation of it, and the version of it in his pub-

[1] A second edition in German type was printed in 1831.

most elementary, being explained to us as we met them in our reading-lessons, and explained with a clearness and emphasis that made it hard to forget them. At the same time he pointed out all that was specially noteworthy in our lessons, and gave us, in English much better than ours, his own translations of passages of peculiar interest or beauty. He bestowed great pains in bringing our untried organs into use in the more difficult details of pronunciation, particularly in the *ö*, the *ü*, the *r*, and the *ch*, on which he took us each separately in hand. His pronunciation was singularly smooth and euphonious. I have been reminded of it in Dresden more than in either Northern or Southern Germany.

Dr. Follen also first introduced gymnastics as a system into Harvard College, certainly of his own motion, and, as I believe, gratuitously. The Delta, where Memorial Hall now stands, was furnished with masts, parallel bars, and the then usual variety of apparatus for athletic training and exercise; and one of the large dining-rooms under the chapel in University Hall was similarly fitted up. We exercised under Dr. Follen's instruction and supervision. He taught us to run with the minimum of fatigue, with the body thrown slightly forward, the arms akimbo, and breathing only through the nose; and he repeatedly led the entire body of students, except the few lame and the fewer lazy, on a run without pause, from the Delta to the top of a hill now crowned by the most conspicuous of the Somerville churches, and back again after a ten minutes' halt. One of my classmates, George F. Haskins (afterward Rev. Father Haskins of the Angel Guardian), so far profited by Dr. Follen's teaching, that, after graduating, he established and conducted a gymnasium at Brown University, and in later years of well and widely known philanthropic service, made thorough gymnastic training a part of his educational system for the poor boys under his charge.

Meanwhile Dr. Follen was attracting attention and interest in various quarters. He lectured on the civil law in Boston, to an audience composed principally of lawyers, who found him an adept in a department of legal science which had then been but little studied in this country. He was subsequently appointed instructor in Ecclesiastical History and Ethics in the Divinity School; and his lectures on ethics were of unsurpassed excellence, both on the score of his scientific knowledge of the ground which they covered, and for the elevated tone of feeling which pervaded them. At the earnest request of Dr. Channing he entered the Christian ministry, and commenced preaching in 1828. I often heard him preach in the college chapel and elsewhere. His sermons were equally instructive and impressive, weighty in thought, full fraught with devotional feeling, written in a style both pure and simple, and delivered with solemnity and earnestness, though without any oratorical adornment.[1] In 1830 he was invited to become pastor of the First Church in Newburyport, and would have accepted the invitation had he not at the same time received what he supposed would be a permanent appointment as Professor of German Literature in Harvard College. He had previously married Miss Eliza Lee Cabot, and about this time he built a house at the corner of the street that now bears his name. His wife was no less lovely in her domestic and social relations, than worthy of high distinction for her literary attainments and ability. Their house was second to no other in Cambridge in all that can make home-life beautiful and lovely. They were "given to hospitality," and no guest failed of the kindest welcome. Indeed, they applied to their guests what in the old arithmetics was termed "the rule of inverse proportion," and showed the most abounding honor, not where such attention could be claimed as a matter of course, but where it was most needed. The reception was simple and unostentatious, but always cordial; and we young men

[1] His failure to pronounce the *th* was the only peculiarity of utterance that would have betrayed him as a foreigner; and his use of the English language was as free from solecisms and inaccuracies as if it had been his vernacular. I can remember but a single mistake of his in the pulpit, and that was in a proper name. It was in the college chapel. His sermon was a spiritualization of some incident in the story of Samson, whom he called *Simson,* as the name is called by the Germans, and as the vowel-points used in the Hebrew Bible would require it to be pronounced. The mistake occasioned no little suppressed mirthfulness.

regarded our perhaps too frequent visits there as among the greatest of our social privileges.

The professorship was supported by a subscription, which expired at the end of five years; and Dr. Follen, having no remaining resource except a small salary as instructor in German, resigned his connection with the college in 1835. He performed some literary labor, and for a while took charge of several private pupils; but the ministry was, for the residue of his life, his chief employment and interest. His zeal in the anti-slavery cause probably prevented his permanent settlement in one of several churches in which he was a favorite preacher. Before resigning his professorship he had taken the lead in the formation of a new religious society in East Lexington; and the members of this society, in 1839, had erected a church edifice, had chosen him as their pastor, and craved his services as a preacher at the dedication, which was appointed for January 15, 1840. In order to meet this engagement, he took passage at New York in the steamer "Lexington," which midway on her route was burned at sea. He was one of the victims. No man can have passed away, more tenderly beloved or more deeply lamented than he was by his pupils and his friends; nor was there any member of our literary community who was held in higher regard for learning profound and varied, and for his thorough work as teacher, lecturer, writer, and preacher.

CHARLES BECK.

(LL.D. 1865.)

Dr. Beck received the degree of Ph.D. at Tübingen. He was the step-son of De Wette, the eminent biblical scholar and critic, and was educated and ordained as a minister in the Lutheran church. He afterward was an instructor in the University of Basle. Implicated in the same designs against autocratic and oppressive rule which made Dr. Follen an exile, and under the same necessity of putting the ocean between himself and the country which he had loved too well, he was Dr. Follen's companion on his voyage to America, and received the same friendly offices on his arrival at New York. He first became a teacher in the Round Hill School at Northampton, and then had a school of his own on the Hudson. In 1832 he was made Professor of Latin in Harvard College, and resigned his office in 1850.

In the class-room Dr. Beck was strict in his requirements, and a rigid disciplinarian, but always just and impartial. He attempted to establish and maintain a high standard of scholarship in his department, and was impatient of inadequate preparation, negligence, and needless failure. His publications were master-works of their kind, but not of a kind to command general interest. The chief of them is a description of the manuscripts of the "Satyricon" of Petronius Arbiter, with a collation of their various readings. Petronius is read by few American scholars, — the fewer the better; but this work is on a level with like monuments of classical erudition that represent the labor of many cloistered years in German universities, and must have renewed the author's early reputation on his native soil. After resigning his professorship, he led a life of which his richly stocked library was the centre, yet with a constant radiation of hospitality, thoughtful kindness, and public service. A hard student by choice and habit, he yet was among the foremost to meet any reasonable demand on his time, labor, or purse; and there was no house in Cambridge where guests found a warmer welcome than with him. The only memorable episode in his quiet life was at the outbreaking of the war of the Rebellion. The ardent patriotism which had driven him from home blazed forth with youthful intensity for the country of his adoption. Not content with doing his full duty as a private citizen, he offered himself for active service, and went into camp, but was discharged by the medical officers of the regiment in which he enlisted, as unfit by reason of his advanced age of sixty-three. He then became an officer of a volunteer military company formed in Cambridge to meet any contingencies of local service, and was throughout the war among the most generous contributors for hospital supplies and sanitary uses. His work in behalf of the Union is gratefully commemorated by a post of the Grand Army that bears his name.

In more peaceful and less public service, Dr. Beck

was a working and much honored member of various literary and scientific associations. He bore a prominent part in the proceedings of the American Oriental Society, and for several years the morning annual meeting of that society in Boston was adjourned for an afternoon and an evening session at his house in Cambridge. He was vice-president of the American Academy of Arts and Sciences. He retained his vigor of body and mind seemingly unimpaired till the last hour of his life, and was riding on horseback, as was his almost daily habit, when he was seized with an apoplectic attack, which had its fatal issue before he could be removed to his own house. He died in 1866.

FRANCIS MARIA JOSEPH SURAULT.

M. SURAULT was appointed instructor in French in Harvard College in 1829, and remained in office nine years. He was a well-educated man, and as good a teacher as he could be with a very imperfect knowledge of the language of his pupils, which I have learned by the observation of many years, both in college and in the outside world, to regard as a disqualification. It is commonly urged in behalf of a (so-called) native teacher of a living tongue, that he is more competent to impart a correct pronunciation than a born American can be. This I doubt. He may, indeed, pronounce his own language better, though it is always possible that his pronunciation may be provincial or plebeian rather than that of the metropolis or the university; but the pupil is not likely to acquire from him so good a pronunciation as from an American who has lived abroad in cultivated society long enough to become familiar with its modes of utterance, and who, nevertheless, will always pronounce the words of another than his native language slowly enough for his pupil's easy imitation. Then, as regards the knowledge of a language as a key to its literature, it is fully as important that the instructor be conversant with his pupil's language as with that which he attempts to teach. This was by no means the case with M. Surault. When I was tutor, he boarded at the same table with me in Commons' Hall, and we were constantly amused by his failure of an adequate English expression of what he wanted to say. Thus, on one occasion, when he came to breakfast with a ruefully sad countenance, and we eagerly inquired the cause, his reply was, "I get a letter that my father has been dead since three months, and I am very much dissatisfied." He wrote a French Grammar, and employed me to correct the proofs. I almost rewrote the book. Whether in so doing I made or marred his fortune, I cannot say. The grammar was in intent and substance excellent, and was used in many schools; but, had it been printed as he wrote it, it might have had a much larger circulation for the grotesque specimens of English that swarmed on every page.

M. Surault was a man of pure and exemplary

character, of a thoroughly kind heart, respected, though inevitably often laughed at, by his pupils, and held in high esteem by his associate teachers.

OLIVER SPARHAWK.

Mr. Sparhawk was appointed steward in 1831, and retained the office till his death in 1835. He belonged to an old family, descended from Rev. John Sparhawk of Salem, and connected by marriage with the Atkinsons of New Hampshire, and with Sir William Pepperell. A gentleman by inheritance, he was equally one in manners and in character. I think that he was already in declining health when I last saw him in 1833; and he died of pulmonary consumption, leaving pleasant memories with all who knew him. Many of his family belonged to the small, amiable, and now almost extinct, sect of Sandemanians, and derived their faith from personal intercourse with its founder. I knew in my early life several members of that communion, all of them persons of superior merit. I feel almost certain that Oliver Sparhawk was classed among them.

JOHN HOOKER ASHMUN.

(1818.)

Mr. Ashmun graduated at the age of eighteen. Shortly after his admission to the bar he became associated with Judge Howe in conducting a law school at Northampton; and, on the ground of his eminent success as a teacher, he was invited to Cambridge on the re-organization of the Law School, to become Judge Story's associate as an instructor, and to be a constantly resident professor, while his senior colleague was necessarily absent for a portion of the time in the exercise of his judicial functions. Mr. Ashmun was already an invalid when he accepted the appointment; and his life in Cambridge, which closed in 1833, was one of growing infirmity and illness, yet of earnest and energetic industry. His disease was pulmonary consumption, which certainly was slower and more insidious in my early days than it has been in these latter years. In his case, I think that he was regarded from the first as under the sentence, and within the shadow, of death. He impressed all who knew him by the sweetness no less than by the strength of his character; and the universal sense of loss and bereavement in his departure was such as seldom attends the death of a young man of however brilliant promise, but rather such as marks the close of a long life of loyal duty and faithful service.

JOHN FESSENDEN.

(1818.)

Mr. Fessenden was a proctor for several years, and a tutor from 1825 to 1827. He was settled for a time as a minister in Deerfield; but, long before his death in 1871, he retired from the active duties of his profession. He was a good scholar and a good man, without any striking qualities of mind or heart that can claim special commemoration.

GEORGE RAPALL NOYES.

(1818.)

Dr. Noyes was a proctor in Harvard College for several years, and then a tutor from 1825 to 1827. He commenced preaching in 1822; but it was understood that he was devoting himself to the critical study of the Scriptures, particularly of the Hebrew Scriptures, and that he therefore chose to remain on university ground, rather than to assume the duties and cares of the active ministry. In 1827, however, he became pastor of a church in Brookfield, and subsequently accepted what he regarded as a more desirable pastorate at Petersham. In both these parishes he left a precious and still enduring memory of faithful service, and of a life which was a continuous preaching of the gospel. But he did not find his fitting place till, in 1840, he returned to Cambridge as Dr. Palfrey's successor in his double professorship, embracing instruction in the Hebrew language and in the exegesis of both the Hebrew and the Christian Scriptures. In these departments, in the judgment of not a few persons conversant with his work, he had no superior among his coevals in America. He was severely honest in his investigations and in the statement of his beliefs. His conclusions were often opposed to his predilections. A conservative by nature, he yet was a pioneer in certain modes and results of criticism which then seemed radical and destructive, and which exposed him to the bitter denunciation of those to whom only the old paths appeared safe, but which now have the suffrage of Christian scholars of every type. I have never known a man so ready as he was to submit whatever he most wanted to believe to the crucial test of research, whether philosophical, historical, or linguistic; and I am glad to record that from this test his faith in the genuineness, integrity, and authenticity of our canonical Gospels, and thus in the alleged facts appertaining to the life, death, and resurrection of Jesus Christ, came forth, as of incontrovertible certainty. It is not surprising that a teacher of a temper and spirit like his should have had in the fullest degree the confidence and reverence of his pupils.

Dr. Noyes published translations of the Book of Job, the Psalms, the Prophets, Proverbs, Ecclesiastes and Canticles, with introductions and critical notes. These versions are unsurpassed in their fidelity to the original, and in simplicity, clearness, and dignity of diction. If they have any fault, it is that they are too literal. Dr. Noyes was not a poet; and his rendering of the Hebrew poets, while immeasurably more intelligible, lacks the rhythmical ring and cadence of our common version; while, of two possible renderings of a psalm or a prophetic rhapsody, he chooses that which is in accordance with prose usage, in preference to the tropical sense which a poet might naturally and probably employ. Yet, with this abatement, I know of no versions of those parts of the Bible which seem to me equal to these as aids to scholarly study.

Dr. Noyes's last work was a translation of the New Testament, in which his double aim was, without setting aside the common version, in the first place to correct its mistranslations, and to substitute current for its few obsolete words and meanings; and, in the second place, to bring the English text into conformity with Tischendorf's then last edition. Subsequent editions and authorities have made a few, yet hardly any important, changes in the Greek text; and I have no hesitation in giving my own opinion, on which, indeed, I have no right to lay any special stress, that Dr. Noyes's is the most faithful and valuable English translation of the New Testament that has ever been made.

As a preacher, Dr. Noyes was sensible, wise, serious, earnest, the master of a pure and chaste English style, but with no superadded ornament, either of rhetoric or of oratory. The intelligent and devout members of a congregation were always instructed and edified by his preaching, but it had little attractive power for those who thought as much of the manner as of the substance of a discourse.

In private and domestic life Dr. Noyes was a man of the beatitudes, rigidly truthful, perseveringly kind, generous in his estimate of the claims and merits of others, helpful in every possible way to those who needed and deserved help. He won the love of all who knew him intimately, no less than the profound respect of all to whom he was known. During the last three or four years of his life he had several severe and protracted illnesses, during which I volunteered my services, not to fill his place, but to occupy it, in the class-room. This, together with my position as pastor of the University Church, brought me into close relations and intercourse with him.

As to religious emotion, he was, for the most part, undemonstrative, except in his cheerful submission to infirmity and suffering. Yet he sometimes spoke of impending death and of the life beyond death with a quiet assurance that indicated the firmness of his faith and trust. At one period of partial convalescence from an attack that threatened a fatal issue, he told me that for several days he had been incapable of continuous thought, but had been made happy by the tacit repetition of the hymns and passages of Scripture which he had learned in childhood under his mother's direction. He said to me but a few days before his death that his earnest prayer had been that he might be spared to complete his work on his version of the New Testament. With a trembling hand, but with his critical judgment clear and keen as ever, he corrected the last proof, and then lay down to die. He lingered a few days longer in peaceful serenity, surrounded by ministries of tender and assiduous love.

His term of office in the Divinity School was twenty-eight years; and a very large proportion of the Unitarian clergy now in advanced or middle life, with some of other denominations almost every year, were trained under his tuition.

WILLIAM FARMER.

(1819.)

Mr. Farmer was for several years a proctor in Harvard College, and then became pastor of a church in Belgrade, Me. He was the tallest man but one that I ever saw, gaunt, grim, and swarthy, with a sepulchral voice, issuing between huge lips from a cavity that yawned like an open sepulchre. Yet he was gentle, meek, humble, and kind, always preferring golden silence to silver speech. He was the subject, to an unlimited extent, of college waggery. An anonymous petition was sent to the proper authorities, praying for blinds on the second-story windows of college-rooms to protect their occupants from Mr. Farmer's scrutiny. Again, at a time when influenza was epidemic in college, and Mr. Farmer's voice in saying grace in Commons' Hall sank into the hoarse sub-bass that indicated him as a sufferer, while for a fortnight or more there was not a ray of clear sunlight, there appeared on the college advertising-board a huge placard, with the announcement in glaring capitals, "The sun has taken his name out [the college phrase for *obtained leave of absence*], having caught the influenza from Farmer."

After leaving college, I saw Mr. Farmer but once; and then he was my guest at Portsmouth. In the days of slow travelling, it was the custom of country ministers to quarter themselves, without invitation or premonition, upon their clerical brethren, — a custom in yielding to which we sometimes "entertained angels unawares;" while we were sometimes less ready to "welcome the coming" than to "speed the parting guest." One evening, when I had been absent from home for an hour or two, I was met at my door by the statement that a man of gigantic stature and fearful mien had arrived with a carpet-bag, and insisted on staying, giving no account of himself, except that I knew him. He had sat in the parlor almost in entire silence, answering what was said to him in gruff monosyllables. I, of course, recognized him, was heartily glad to see him, and paid him the respect due, if not to his unsightly outer man, to his sterling excellence. This may have been in 1837. Of his subsequent fortunes I know nothing. I learn from the catalogue that he was admitted to the degree of A.M. (probably *ad eundem*) at Yale College in 1843, and that he died in 1862.

JAMES HAYWARD.

(1819.)

Mr. Hayward had a strange life-story. Born in extreme poverty, he was, at different times, a servant in the family of Deacon Walley of Boston, a truckman, a laborer in a brickyard, the keeper of a huckster's shop. A younger brother, Rev. Tilly Brown

Hayward (H. U., 1820), somehow started in the pursuit of a liberal education. James was seized with ambition to take a similar course, and so availed himself of his brother's books and aid as to enter college a year before him. He held a high rank in his class, and the year after his graduation was appointed Tutor in Mathematics. By six years' service, like Mr. Otis, he earned a professorship, and like him, under the Salem administration, was suffered to hold it but a single year. Meanwhile he was licensed as a preacher, and preached well, but seldom. After resigning his professorship, he became a civil engineer, and had charge of the construction of the earliest sections of the Boston and Maine Railroad, of which he afterward was president. He accumulated what in his time was regarded as an ample fortune, and bequeathed twenty thousand dollars to the Harvard College Observatory.

Mr. Hayward was never ashamed of his early history; indeed, seemed to regard it with an honest pride. When my classmate, the late Hon. Samuel H. Walley, entered college, Mr. Hayward called upon him, and, pointing to the fireplace, said, "Walley, I used to clean those andirons." He was once invited to preach in the Representatives' Chamber at Washington; and, with the announcement of the name and office of the preacher for the day, there were inquiries concerning him at the hotel breakfast-table at which he was seated. There were present two or three New-England members of Congress, who had heard of him, and told what they knew of his early days; and, said Mr. Hayward, "I corrected some of their statements, and added others." One of them invited him to go to the service with him. He accepted the invitation, but, instead of taking the seat which his new friend offered him, gave that friend the first intimation of his actual name and position by acknowledging his courtesy by a bow, and passing on to the Speaker's desk.

With reference to Mr. Hayward's relation to his pupils, I have a theory which I do not share with my surviving classmates. In his time, there was as little interchange of friendly offices between the Faculty and the students as there used to be between Jews and Samaritans. On the side of the Faculty Mr. Hayward's conduct was exceptional. He evidently sought opportunities or pretexts for going into students' rooms. He would beg a shovelful of coals to kindle his fire, or would light his lamp at that of an opposite neighbor;[1] while his fellow-tutors would rather have spent the night in cold and darkness, or have worn their fingers to the bone in the vain endeavor to elicit a spark from the flint and steel.

[1] This was before the invention of lucifer matches, when in a respectable house the fire was never suffered to go out, and when a lamp was lighted either by blowing a coal into a blaze with the breath, or by the use of offensive brimstone matches. The office of the Vestal Virgins only represented the need of perennial fire which was everywhere recognized and felt. Cicero enumerates among the common obligations between man and man the permission to light fire from fire.

The universal belief was, that Mr. Hayward's visits were with a view to espionage. But I never knew of his seeing any thing that was unfit for a tutor to see, or of any mischief to a student in consequence of his domiciliary visits; and my belief is, that they grew from a sincere and honest wish to break down the traditionary barrier, and to establish such a relation as now subsists between the once opposite parties to their mutual pleasure and profit. I am confirmed in this opinion by impressions derived from my subsequent intercourse with him, which was suspended only by his death in 1866.

JOHN PORTER.

(1819.)

Mr. Porter was assistant-librarian when I entered college, and died in 1825. He was the son of Rev. Huntington Porter (H. U., 1777) of Rye, N.H., and nephew of Rev. Dr. Porter of Roxbury, who took charge of his education. He became a preacher in 1822, but was not often in the pulpit. His reputation was that of a man of respectable ability, good scholarship, and blameless and exemplary character.

NATHANIEL GAGE.

(1822.)

Mr. Gage was tutor for the academic year 1825–26, and was afterward a pastor of churches successively in Nashua, Haverhill, and Westborough. He was a man of superior scholarship, and of the most amiable character. Had he thought as well of himself as his friends thought of him, he would have held a commanding place in his profession and in society; but his diffidence and self-distrust prevented him from ever doing himself full justice, or winning all the reputation that he deserved. No man can have been more beloved than he, or more worthily.

WILLIAM PARSONS LUNT.

(1823.)

Dr. Lunt served as proctor in college for a year or two, then became minister of the Second Unitarian Church in New York, and afterward of the First Church in Quincy, where he had among the constant attendants on his services and his warmest friends and admirers, John Quincy and Charles Francis Adams. He was distinguished for sound, clear, and vigorous thought, for a rare wealth of imaginative power, and for a style of singular purity and beauty. He was a poet, too, and some of his sacred lyrics have a permanent place in various hymnals. He had great reputation as a preacher, but shunned rather than sought publicity, and thus was seldom heard out of his own pulpit. Yet there were occasions on which he could not evade the distinction which he so fully merited. His sermon on the two-hundredth anniversary of his church was unsurpassed, if not unequalled, in its kind. His discourse at the interment of John Quincy Adams was largely circulated, and was universally regarded as the most just, discriminating, and eloquent of the many tributes to his memory. His address delivered before the Divinity School at Cambridge, and his Dudleian Lecture, were master-works of Christian philosophy and scholarship. He died in Arabia, on a journey to Palestine, in 1857.

GEORGE RIPLEY.

(1823.)

George Ripley was tutor for the academic year 1825–26, and then became the first pastor of the Thirteenth Congregational Church in Boston, — a church established in Purchase Street, in a quarter of the city where there was then a large Protestant population, with no small number of persons of wealth and high social standing, and of old family mansions occupied generally by the descendants of their original owners. His ministry of fifteen years was not otherwise than prosperous, though before its close the character of the population in the neighborhood of his church had already sensibly changed; and under his successor the site was abandoned for one which soon afterward became equally unsuitable. Mr. Ripley early adopted the philosophico-religious views which were known, or rather unknown, under that most vague of all terms, — *transcendental*, — and was involved in a controversy with Professor Norton, not as to the fact of the supernatural element in Christianity, but as to its evidential value or validity.

that, had I the power, I could reproduce them from memory. They were suggestive of more than earthly music; and, were there literally songs of angels, their melody could be not unlike his. He sang in the college chapel. The little organ in the chapel was an English one, with few stops, but with marvellously rich tones; and it was then played by Cooper, who was second to no organist of his time. There were several other fine voices in the choir. Joseph Angier (H. U., 1828) was a member of the choir in Brigham's senior year, and they sang together the tenor and alto duets which abounded in the tunes then in vogue. There was one of those tunes called "Clifford,"—probably of unscientific harmony, else it would not have fallen out of use, but with a charming melody,—of which I can, after all these years, rehearse the duets to the inward ear as distinctly as if I had heard it but yesterday. Mr. Brigham had a moral and spiritual nature as finely strung as were the chords that made his ear so true and his voice so sweet. With a countenance that betokened the utmost purity and delicacy of character, and equally a quick and clear intellect, he was feeble and slender, and looked as if he might fade away easily and early. Indeed, there was in his rendering of sacred music some suggestion of the swan-song; and no one that knew him in his best estate supposed that he could live long. He studied for the ministry, and undoubtedly preached, though I know not when or where. The catalogue registers his death as in 1831.

SAMUEL KIRKLAND LOTHROP.

(1825.)

Dr. Lothrop held the office of proctor for a year or two while he was in the Divinity School. He was a grandson of Rev. Samuel Kirkland, the missionary to the Indians, and a nephew, and virtually the adopted son, of President Kirkland. In his uncle's family he had rare privileges of social intercourse. Though not distinguished as a scholar while in college, he had, and retained through life, the faculty of imbibing without effort, almost unconsciously, whatever was best worth remembering, whether in books, formal discourse, or conversation. In the Divinity School he was a close, earnest, and faithful student; and with unusual attractions of manners, of capacity as a writer, and of oratorical power, he gave no uncertain presage of success in his profession. His first settlement in the ministry was as pastor of a new Unitarian Church in Dover, N.H., where he had among his hearers a large proportion of the prominent men and the best families in the town, and, while admired as a preacher, won the enduring respect and affection of the people under his charge. In 1834, at the age of thirty, he became minister of the church in Brattle Square, Boston. Here he fully met the demands of a congregation that had enjoyed the services of a series of clergymen whose fame had become historical. At the same time he performed a vast amount of labor outside of his own parish. He was for many years a member of the school committee, and is believed to have devoted more time, thought, and care to the work than any other member, being generally the chairman of important sub-committees, and instituting by his elaborate reports numerous improvements in administration and discipline, while at the same time always ready to give the teachers his advice and sympathy. He was a leader in various charitable enterprises, both secular and religious, and was president or secretary of more benevolent societies than can be easily numbered; such trusts being never with him sinecures, but always discharged promptly, thoroughly, and efficiently. He was constantly beset by applicants for counsel and aid, from whom, when deserving, his kindness was never withholden; while he had so quick and keen an insight into character, that he was hardly ever imposed upon.

With advancing years, there was no decline in Dr. Lothrop's power as a preacher, or in the attachment and interest of the families that remained under his pastoral care. His church would have been alive to-day, had its members thought that it could die. But the place of worship, once central, genteel, and quiet, gradually came to be surrounded by hotels, stables, and old-clothes' shops; while it was within easy reach of hardly any of the parishioners. Of course, in such a site, there were no new-comers to supply the place of the families disintegrated by death, or lost by removal. When at length those who continued to worship in the old church discovered that they were very few, they resolved, but too late, to build a new church edifice. While this was in building, several of the most important members of the congregation died; and, when it was completed, its acoustic properties were such as to render speaking and hearing equally difficult. Under these discouraging circumstances, the society was disbanded, and virtually dissolved.

For his few remaining years Dr. Lothrop led an industrious life, often re-appearing in the pulpit, using his ready pen to good purpose, and enjoying in full the tokens of respect and affection that were the chief incidents of each passing day. No man can have been more, or more worthily, endeared and cherished than he was in the love of family, kindred, and more friends than could be numbered, or can have left a memory richer in the many diverse and resplendent traits and habits of spirit and of life that are comprised in that highest of all titles, — the Christian gentleman.

ALLEN PUTNAM.

(1825.)

Mr. Putnam was a proctor while in the Divinity School. He probably was a teacher for two years after leaving college, and commenced preaching in 1830. He was settled as minister of the Unitarian Church in Augusta, Me. After nine or ten years he resigned his charge, and, I think, then ceased to preach. I lost knowledge of him for many years; and, when I renewed my acquaintance with him, he was in the wood and coal business in Roxbury. Of late he has been a hierophant among the (so-called) spiritualists, a frequent speaker at their meetings, the author of a commentary on the Gospels in accordance with their theories, and, if not the author, the editor, of very numerous letters, purporting to be communications from distinguished men, no longer living in this world, containing self-accusations for their willing blindness, or for conduct opposed to their unwilling convictions, with reference to divers manifestations of necromancy. While I am not disposed to receive these documents as authentic, and yet am unable to solve the curious problem in psychology which they present, I still believe Mr. Putnam to have been an honest man, self-deluded, and free from all conscious wrong in his assaults on the fair fame of the dead and the credulity of the living. Just as I was preparing to write this notice of him, I saw the announcement of his death.

JOHN LANGDON SIBLEY.

(1825.)

No form is more identified with Harvard College in the memory of hundreds of graduates than that of Mr. Sibley. Of the eighty-one years of his life, sixty were spent in Cambridge, — forty-four as a member of the University, and thirty-seven in its official service; while with the title of Librarian Emeritus, conferred on him when he could no longer perform the active duties which were his delight, his name appeared in fifty annual catalogues. His father was a physician in Union, Me., with excellent reputation, both professional and personal, and with a practice more extensive than gainful. He craved a liberal education for his eldest son; and, learning of the beneficiary provision at Exeter for students of promise, he sought this aid to supplement his own slender resources. Of the sacrifices that he made in his son's behalf, some estimate may be formed from his having postponed the purchase of his first pair of spectacles, after he had begun to need them, in order to furnish his son with the means of buying a Greek lexicon. Young Sibley must have maintained a blameless character and a high standard of scholarship at Exeter, else he would have been dropped from the foundation, which, from the first, has never given a foothold to youth who could not, or would not, do it honor. He entered college at the age of seventeen, was a close student, held a high rank in his class, and received honorable appointments at both junior and senior exhibitions, and on graduating. At the same time he provided in various ways for his own support, in his first year as president's freshman, with the duty of carrying messages and notes on college business from the president to officers and members of the college; in subsequent years, probably by keeping a winter school, in accordance with the general custom of all the students who were not from local histories and rare editions, were discovered by his enterprise; and not a few of the most valuable benefactions were elicited by such friendly attentions and kindnesses on his part as gave good promise of fruitful returns. He also edited the Annual Catalogue of the college for twenty years, and prepared no less than ten Triennial Catalogues, which required constant vigilance and extensive correspondence throughout the years intervening between each and the following issue, and which, under his hands, attained a degree of accuracy entirely unprecedented. For fifteen years, too, he issued, on Commencement week, a complete Harvard Necrology, including under each name such salient dates and facts in the life-record as reached him by means of information which he kept in constant employment, and from which he made and preserved copious minutes.

But Mr. Sibley's greatest and most enduring service to the college is his "Biographical Sketches of Graduates of Harvard College." Of this work he completed three large octavo volumes; the third volume including the class of 1689, and brought to a close with the last remnant of working-power which remained to him from the incessant toil of nearly fourscore years. This labor was performed under what to many men would have seemed physical inability. He was operated upon for cataract in both eyes at different times; and, though these operations were reckoned as successful, his restoration was by no means so complete as to render the consulting of unfamiliar manuscripts, ill-printed documents, and matter sometimes almost illegible, otherwise than painful and intensely wearisome. Yet he left no source of information without drawing from it all that it could furnish, and was careful to reproduce whatever he transcribed, in all the minutiæ of spelling, punctuation, capitals, and Italics, with literal exactness. The work could not have been better done, nor so well by any other man, nor yet at a later time; for the memorials, written and traditional, of our colonial days are constantly dropping out of sight and out of mind; and so fast an age as ours is as prone to forget, as our fathers were solicitous to remember, the past. The time is not far distant when these volumes will be the sole extant authority for a large proportion of their contents; and, sent down to coming generations with the seal of authenticity which our own impresses upon them, they will have a growing interest and value as long as the college shall stand.

In 1860 Mr. Sibley's father died, leaving to him, his only surviving child, the entire savings of his long life of self-denying industry, with the one exception of a legacy of a hundred dollars to Phillips Exeter Academy. The property thus left amounted to less than five thousand dollars. Mr. Sibley gave the whole of it to the academy, and subsequently added more than twice that sum, creating a fund which, by his provision, was to accumulate under certain prescribed conditions and limitations. A part of the income of this fund is already in use, while the capital amounts to more than forty thousand dollars. Mr. Sibley directed that his name should be strictly concealed, but was induced, in the hope that other benefactors might be won by his example, to permit the secret to be divulged at an academic festival in 1872. On that occasion Dr. Palfrey presided. Mr. Sibley was present, and, when the announcement was made, was forced upon his feet by shouts of applause. In a speech of rare *naïveté*, pathos, and unstudied eloquence, with a modesty and filial piety that disclaimed all praise for himself, and won from all who heard him the most reverent regard for his parents, he told the story of his early life, of his native home, and of the patient and loving toil and sacrifice of those to whose memory he wished to dedicate the Sibley fund. Of his gift he made small account: but this speech, probably the only speech of any length that he ever made, remained with him the great event of his life; and he never ceased to congratulate himself on its success.

In Mr. Sibley's character, integrity bore a conspicuous part; and by this I do not mean mere honesty in the narrower sense of the word, but also conscientious accuracy, truthfulness and justice, in all the details of thought, word, and deed. He would be lavish of time, and of money if need were, in determining an obscure date, or the proper orthography of an unimportant name, simply because he deemed it wrong to state what he did not know, or to omit, in any work which he undertook, the full statement of all that he could know.

Closely economical in personal expenditure, Mr. Sibley was generous to every one but himself. Many poor students owed to him their ability to remain on college-ground. There were persons who for years depended on such subsidies as he gave them to eke out their slender income. From his home and table, poor homes and meagrely spread tables received liberal supplies. His hospitality was often extended for weeks and months to those whose only claim was their need. Without parade or ostentation he welcomed every opportunity for doing good; and I doubt whether there was ever a year, for the last half of his life, when he did not spend more for others than for himself. It was a characteristic trait that he gave special directions that his funeral should be as simple and inexpensive as was consistent with propriety, and that the amount thus saved should be given to the poor.

In his home-life, which began not till 1866, he accounted himself, and with good reason, pre-eminently happy; his wife having been in full sympathy with him in his benevolent purposes, and still deeming it her happiness to employ the income of his estate in precisely the offices of kindness and charity which it was his joy to render.[1] As a friend, he was

[1] Mrs. Sibley, who has become a resident of Groton, on leaving Cambridge gave the house and estate in Phillips Place, bought by her at the time of her marriage, and thus her own separate property, to the Cambridge Hospital.

true and loyal. In dress, manners, appearance, and personal habits, he preserved, to the last, much of the simplicity, and many of the unconventional ways, of his rural birthplace and his early life: but there was in him the very soul of courtesy; and those who knew him best had often fresh surprises in his fineness and delicacy of feeling, his tenderness for the sensibility of others, and his choice of such modes of performing kind acts as might best keep himself in the background, and ward off the painful sense of obligation.

The last few months of Mr. Sibley's life were a season of debility and suffering, with few and brief intervals of relief. In the early summer of 1885, there was a slight improvement; and he cherished a strong hope that he might be able to officiate as chorister in the singing of St. Martin's at the Commencement dinner, — an office which, as the successor of Dr. Pierce, he had filled for thirty-six years. But, as the day approached, he became himself aware, as those about him had been previously, that such an effort was beyond his ability. From that time he was confined for the most part to his room, and gradually lost his hold on passing events and his interest in the outside world. The closing hour often seemed very near; but with a natively strong constitution, unimpaired by luxury, indulgence, or indolence, he resisted and overcame repeated paroxysms of disease that threatened an immediately fatal issue. His illness had every alleviation and comfort that could be afforded by the most assiduous, skilful, and loving

Meadville, Penn., as a teacher in the Huidekoper family, and a minister of the then infant Unitarian Church in that town. He died there in 1833. His was the first death in my class, which appeared in two Triennial Catalogues without a star.

HERSEY BRADFORD GOODWIN.

(1826.)

MR. GOODWIN was a proctor during a part of his course in the Divinity School, which he entered immediately on graduating. He was round-shouldered, of less than the average stature, and probably of a naturally feeble constitution; but his eye, face, and manner indicated a superior vigor and quickness of mind and a winning character. He held a high rank as a scholar, yet without making rank a special object of endeavor. He was a great favorite with our whole class, though without any of the arts by which popularity is commonly sought. In his boyhood he was so pure and true that his step-mother, a Calvinist of the old school, used to say, "It does seem to me that Hersey is one who never fell;" and with the same unsullied mien and conduct in college, he mingled in all of fun and frolic that was blameless, while it was well understood that there were limits beyond which he could not be induced to go.

After declining an invitation to settle in Rochester, N.Y., Mr. Goodwin, in 1830, became colleague pastor with Rev. Dr. Ripley of the First Church in Concord, Mass., where, after the lapse of more than half a century since his death, his name is still familiar and precious. His senior in the charge of the church loved him as if he had been his own son. Mr. Goodwin was a singularly attractive preacher; and when the church in Brattle Square became vacant, on the resignation of Dr. Palfrey, he was earnestly requested to preach there for a Sunday, of course in the thought of the committee as an eligible candidate for settlement. I doubt whether he would have been willing to leave Concord; but he might have accepted an invitation that would not have compromised him, had it not been for the strong remonstrance of Dr. Ripley, who was indignant that the thought of stealing his colleague should have entered the minds of the Boston committee, and who begged to be permitted to answer the letter, saying, "I will give them a Sunday; and it will be such a Sunday as they never had before, and will never want to have again." In the second year of his pastorate Mr. Goodwin was bereaved of his wife, in less than a year and a half after their marriage. While he sustained this bereavement with firmness and resignation, it was too severe for his physical frame, which can never have been strong. For the remaining five years of his life, he was subject to attacks of what was or became a disease of the heart. With several enforced intervals of rest, he still performed for most of the time his full amount of labor in the pulpit and in pastoral service, and but two days before his death seemed convalescent. After a day pleasantly spent with his

Unitarian pulpit at the national capital. Dr. Hosmer, however, rightly preferred to remain at Buffalo; and I believe that it would have been for his happiness, had he declined a subsequent invitation to become president of Antioch College, which he accepted in 1866. This institution was never properly endowed, and, when he took the charge of its interests, had a much smaller amount of funds that could be made available than appeared on its books, or than it possessed in the imagination of its sanguine friends. During the seven years of Dr. Hosmer's term of office, he was obliged to devote a large portion of his time and energy to the financial needs of the college; and it required all the prestige of his established reputation to prop up its declining fortunes. He, however, did good service there, was respected and beloved by teachers and students, and resigned his charge before its burdens had become too heavy for his elastic strength and his optimistic temperament. Then followed the most remarkable period of his life. In his seventieth year he assumed the pastorate of the Channing Church in Newton, Mass., and for at least six years was as vigorous in body and mind, in writing and in utterance, in pastoral labor and in conversational power, and especially in his influence upon the young and his strong hold on the children of his charge, as he had been in early or middle life. His society became so warmly attached to him, that when at length he asked to be released, as unable to perform the full work to which he had been accustomed, they insisted on diminishing the amount of his labor rather than lose his services altogether. After a ministry of nine years, however, he resigned his pastorate to a successor, till whose installation he still performed all the pastoral duties of a large parish, and met many calls for service in the surrounding community. The remaining two years of his life were a period of infirmity and decline.

GEORGE PUTNAM.

(1826.)

My classmate Putnam was a very high scholar in college, and was then thought as much of by his classmates as in after-life in the outside world. He was not ambitious of rank. We supposed, perhaps rightly, that, if he had been so, he would have led the class. As the case was, he held the fifth or sixth place. The difference between that and the first place was, perhaps, due to one habit in which he persisted. We then had, normally, three recitations a day, — one before breakfast, a second late in the forenoon, a third late in the afternoon; and the only convenient time for learning the morning lesson was the preceding evening, which by many of the students was prolonged till or beyond midnight. Putnam always went to bed at nine o'clock; and while he generally spent a sufficient part of the evening in study, if he was prevented from so doing, the morning lesson suffered. He was among the youngest of the class, entering college at the age of sixteen; but he was thoroughly manly in self-control and independence, in fully formed and impregnable principle, and in fixed opinions on all those great subjects that underlie character and conduct. I think that any indiscretion, folly, or wrong-doing would have been as entirely unexpected, and would have seemed as unnatural, in him at seventeen as at seventy. On graduating he kept school for a year in Duxbury. It was his intention, after a year or two so spent, to return to Sterling, his native town, and to live on a farm which he had inherited, and which in after-years was his wonted summer resort. But Rev. Henry Ware, junior, aware of his rare ability and merit, was unwilling that the church should lose his active service, and was at special pains, not without difficulty, to urge him to enter the Divinity School. While there, he filled for a part of the time the office of proctor.

In 1830 Mr. Putnam was ordained as associate pastor with Rev. Dr. Porter, of the First Religious Society in Roxbury, then a rural parish, large, indeed, rich, and with many distinguished men and families on its roll, but approachable from Boston only by the narrow "Neck" and through a thinly settled suburb. The parish grew faster than the village, and the church had become metropolitan before Roxbury was entitled to claim a city charter. During the greater part of Dr. Putnam's ministry, there were not a few residents of Boston proper who attended his church, even before the time of easy transit. There might seem to be no need of my saying any thing about the preaching of one whose primacy in the pulpit was so universally recognized, and yet I want to give my own opinion as to the secret of his power. His sermons were in one sense not elaborate, while in another sense they could not have been more elaborate than they were. I do not believe that he ever concerned himself about style. With his taste and culture, his diction could not have been otherwise than pure, perspicuous, and elegant. With his directness of aim and purpose, it was of necessity forceful. But while he could safely leave his sentences to take care of themselves, he was an industrious thinker, with rare power of thought, and of thought both deep and clear; and his mind was intensely occupied on the great themes, religious and ethical, which had their counterpart in his own consciousness, and which he contemplated in their bearing on the community and on individual character. Thus, in what seemed his leisure hours, — nay, to one who did not know him, his seasons of repose and indolence, — he was creating materials for those sermons, which he wrote or dictated at small expense of time and with no apparent effort, yet which were an intense motive power, and "a power working for righteousness," to the congregations that never failed to crowd his church, and to hang upon his words, and to which he seemed, and in their memory still seems, unequalled, if not unapproached. In fact, he did not, in the hackneyed phrase, "study" his sermons; but they were the natural and inevitable effluence of his own mind and soul. In like manner, we may account for what was unique in his delivery. He had no oratorical arts or rules or habits. His speech in the pulpit was as plain and unartistical as his common conversation. Yet the most accomplished elocutionist could not have read his sermons so impressively and efficiently as he delivered them. They were in themselves sermons that would have done much of their work, had they been barely read; but in delivering them, he somehow put into them, in voice, mien, and manner, all the stress and vividness of conviction and emotion in which they had been written; and his hearers felt, in listening to him, as if they were looking right into his soul. Then, too, though he seldom or never entered the pulpit without his manuscript, he was not confined to it, or limited by it; and his unwritten words were sometimes the part of his sermon that took the firmest grasp on the consciences of his audience.

Dr. Putnam was pre-eminently a wise counsellor and faithful helper to the people under his charge, having their loyal affection, and, still more, their entire confidence. He had a discretion never at fault in the management of secular concerns; and while he left the charge of his own interests to a friend who relieved him of care and responsibility, he gave his advice and aid not infrequently to those in need of judicious counsel in the management of their affairs. He was for many years a member of the Corporation of Harvard College, and, in that capacity, rendered to the University a large amount of arduous and faithful service. For two years he represented the Roxbury district in the Legislature, in which he served on important committees, and was heard with interest and profound respect on all such measures appertaining to the general good as were, or ought to have been, outside of the range of party politics.

In 1873 Dr. Putnam had an attack of paralysis, from which he partially recovered, so far as to reappear sometimes in the pulpit with no apparent failure in preaching power, and certainly with none in mental grasp and capacity, and he officiated in his wonted manner on several more private occasions; but the five remaining years of his life were a season of growing infirmity, with occasional intermissions of seeming convalescence, but with alternating periods of weakness and decline. He retained to the last clear self-consciousness, and marked with cheerful serenity the stages by which he passed from the waning earthly life to the life of heaven.

OLIVER STEARNS.

(1826.)

THE fifth classmate on my list. He was the nephew of Professor Asahel Stearns, and inherited similar family traits. Entering college at the age of fifteen, he held the second place in his class, and distinguished himself particularly in mathematics, which formed then a much larger portion of the curriculum than in later years. On graduating, he became usher in Mr. Greene's school at Jamaica Plain, and then entered the Divinity School in 1827, at the same time receiving, and holding for two years, an appointment as tutor in mathematics. As to his tutorship, our class-secretary makes the laconic entry, "Popular, yet windows broken;" the first statement being at that time exceptional, the latter normal. In 1830 he was ordained as pastor of the Unitarian Church in Northampton, where he was successful and happy, but in feeble health, and advised to seek a residence near the sea. This he found at Hingham, where he was minister of the Third Congregational Society, and won the undivided respect and affection of the whole community. He went thence to become president of the Meadville Divinity School; and the ability manifested and the reputation gained in that office designated him as the man fitted beyond all others to fill the Professorship of Pulpit Eloquence and Pastoral Care in the Cambridge Divinity School, made vacant in 1863 by the death of Dr. Francis.

Dr. Stearns's character is difficult to describe from its lack of perspective, — from the absence of faults and defects that can throw the traits of excellence into high relief. He had the virtues in such relative equilibrium that it is hard to name any prominent characteristic. Faithful in every charge; diligent in duty; calm and trustful under as severe trials as can fall to the lot of any man; generous, kind, and helpful in every relation; unostentatiously, yet profoundly, religious; in the best sense living above the world, while he never forgot how he ought to live in it,—he lacked not the love of all who knew him well; but their reverence even exceeded their affection for him. As a preacher, he held and deserved a reputation among the foremost, during his two pastorates, and until the pressure of academic work made him feel, and therefore seem, as a stranger in the pulpit. His preaching was pre-eminently spiritual; and while he could not easily come down to his hearers, he had the rarer faculty of bringing them up to him, and making them earnest listeners to such sermons as would gain little attention from the stated hearers of (so-called) popular preachers. He left an unspeakably precious record in the homes and hearts of his parishioners; and those of them who survive recall his life among them with as fresh, vivid, and loving memory as if the years of separation had been but days. With retired and studious habits, of few words where words were not needed, with little taste or capacity for the ordinary forms and occasions of social intercourse, he yet entered with the most prompt, tender, and helpful sympathy into the cares, griefs, and joys of his flock, was their closest friend in every stress of need, and spoke to them with the authority and power of one whose mission was from heaven.

Dr. Stearns was also a pioneer in the reforms in which zeal was as hazardous to one's reputation, as indifference became in later years. Especially in the anti-slavery cause, he took the cross and bore the reproach, while the New-England pulpit was, for the most part, silent or antagonistic. He was too thoroughly a Christian to give utterance to abuse or invective; but his was among the most earnest voices in urging on Northern men their duty and responsibleness as to slavery, in demonstrating their complicity in its wrongs and sins, and in exposing the time-serving and sycophancy of men in place and power.

In his relations to the divinity schools that enjoyed his services, it is impossible to over-estimate the extent, accuracy, and thoroughness of his scholarship, and his unwearying devotion to his work. The most exhaustive treatment of the subject in hand was his rule and method. His courses of instruction comprehended a singularly wide range of topics: yet he never appeared in the lecture-room without ample preparation, and full command of the ground before him; and he rather oppressed his pupils by the affluence and redundancy of his resources, than left them at any time to feel that his treatment fell short of what his subject demanded.

Dr. Stearns never recovered the bodily vigor which wilted during his first pastorate. With the feebleness of an invalid he performed the full tale of work that belonged to a strong man. But in 1878 he found himself unable for further labor, and resigned his professorship. He lived seven years longer. His decline was very gradual; and he faded away without acute disease or suffering, and even with no token of the very near approach of death.

EDMUND CUSHING.

(1827.)

EDMUND CUSHING'S mother was a sister of Asahel, and an aunt of Oliver, Stearns; and on his father's side he belonged to a family of superior ability and position. His elder brother, Judge Luther Stearns Cushing, was the author of Cushing's "Manual," — which, I believe, is still of authority in the conduct of deliberative assemblies, — and of certain legal works of acknowledged merit. The younger brother was among the brightest men and best scholars of his class. I had no intimacy with him, and I remember him chiefly as having been the college organist for several years. He had an ability as a musical performer that was literally peculiar. I cannot describe it; but, had I command of the requisite knowledge and skill, I am sure that I could reproduce it. It has left in my memory the impression of a wonderfully light, almost airy, touch of the keys, yet with strong stress on such notes or strains as claimed special emphasis. If I may employ for sound a word belonging to sight, his playing was the most picturesque that I ever heard. I believe that it was regarded with favor by musical authorities: it certainly charmed me.

Mr. Cushing was tutor for a year. He settled as

a lawyer in Charlestown, N.H., and acquired high distinction at the bar. He was for several of the last years of his life Chief Justice of the Supreme Court. After his removal from Cambridge I saw him but twice. Once he spent an evening with me at my house in Portsmouth. Many years afterward I went to Charlestown to preach at an ordination, and was his guest. I did not see him during the public service, and the last thing that would have occurred to me was that the Chief Justice of the State was presiding at the organ. Yet on my return to his house, I said to him, "There was something in the way in which the organ was handled this evening, that reminded me of your playing years and years ago in the college chapel." His reply was, "No wonder, for you have been hearing me;" and he told me that he had always been the organist in that church, except when absent on professional duty.

CORNELIUS CONWAY FELTON.

(1827.)

I WAS examined for admission to college with the class of 1827, and, studying at home through the ensuing year, entered the class of 1826 at the Commencement next following. In the section, not exceeding five, in which I was examined, the thirteenth in numerical order, I met Felton; and we interchanged our hopes and fears as to the issue of the day, and talked together while we were in waiting at the doors of the examiners, and as we stood outside of the president's study, while the twelve preceding sections received in succession the award of the Faculty. When I returned to Cambridge the following year, though in different classes, we met as friends, and saw each other not infrequently. At a later period we were fellow-teachers in college; and from that time, though living apart for many years, we were closely intimate, and, as I have no reason to doubt, with the strong affection on his part which existed on mine. Indeed, I undoubtedly owed my professorship to his personal regard, my appointment having been made at the first meeting of the Corporation at which he presided.

Mr. Felton inherited from his parents superior intelligence and moral worth, but was indebted to friends who saw his early promise for the aid and encouragement in the pursuit of a liberal education which his father was unable to render. He was distinguished in college for his power of rapid acquisition, his scholarly tastes, and his proficiency in the Latin, and especially in the Greek, language and literature, in which last he was not only recognized as the first scholar among his coevals, but left the second far behind him. Indeed, before he graduated, his life-work seemed to be marked out for him.

Immediately on graduating, he went to Geneseo, N.Y., to take charge, with two of his classmates, of a classical school then recently established. After two years he returned to Cambridge as tutor in Greek, became College Professor of Greek in 1832, and succeeded Dr. Popkin as Eliot Professor of Greek Literature in 1834. In the academic year, 1832–33, I was a tutor in mathematics, and lived in Hollis. Felton had taken the room in Holworthy which Dr. Popkin had occupied for many years. He and I, as in college age the oldest of the parietal officers, had the chief charge of the police of the college-yard; and in one respect we instituted a new method, attended by the desired result. Bonfires had been of frequent occurrence in the college-yard. Petroleum had not then been discovered, nor were tar-barrels easily procured; but the fires were made of honest wood from the students' own wood-piles. The chief object of these fires was, undoubtedly, to bring out the *posse* of parietal officers in chase of the noisy groups, that scattered when they were approached, and dodged the dark-lantern[1] when the slide was removed and the light almost flashed upon the offender's face. We determined to direct our attention in such cases to the fire, and not to the students. We pulled the ignited sticks apart; and, when the fire was thus arrested, we conveyed the fuel to our own rooms. After two or three experiments, the students grew tired of furnishing kindling-wood to their teachers; and the wonted blaze and outcry ceased for the rest of the year.

For thirty years Mr. Felton instructed college-

[1] The rooms of the tutors and proctors were at that time fully furnished by the college, and dark-lanterns were among the essential items of furniture.

classes in Greek, and for twenty-six years was at the head of the department. In the class-room he was the opposite of rigid and exacting, and an indifferent scholar was put by him under no compulsory pressure; but those who were ready to learn received from him the most ample aid, and derived from their intercourse with him the strongest stimulus to persevering industry. Indeed, such students as were disposed to love classical literature were drawn to him by an elective affinity; and, as he reached and passed middle life, there were always among the *habitués* of his house, and his intimate associates, those many years his juniors, with whom he grew young again in their common enthusiasm for Greece and its monuments. At the same time his genial disposition and his fellow-feeling with young life, which never waned, made him a favorite teacher, even with those who profited the least by his instruction.

When the presidency of the college became vacant by the resignation of Dr. Walker in 1860, Mr. Felton was not only chosen as his successor, but was designated by all the friends of the college as the only man who should or could be chosen. In this office it can hardly be said that he met, but he very far transcended, the expectations of his friends. They thought that he would fill the office with dignity and grace, and adorn it by the breadth, thoroughness, and fame of his liberal culture; and herein they were not disappointed. But they hardly expected that he would take upon himself in full the unnumbered details of prosaic duty and service which then made the presidency of Harvard University as multifarious a charge as could well be devised or imagined. Yet with an intense feeling of responsibility he entered upon a singularly energetic administration, mastering all the details of the office, taking cognizance of the work of all the teachers, and making himself felt in every department, not merely as a gracious presence, but as an efficient force. He even became, when there was need, a strict disciplinarian; though, in the infliction of censure and penalty, he evidently felt more pain than he gave.

I entered on my duties as professor simultaneously with his assuming the presidential chair, and my first official service was as chaplain at his inauguration. We met daily, at morning prayers; and, unless the weather were very inclement, we walked together after the service, up and down the college-paths, for fifteen or twenty minutes, or longer, oftener than not talking over the college concerns which, for the time, were giving him trouble or solicitude. I could see that his work was wearing upon him, and that the incessant strain and tension were more than he could bear. Symptoms of heart-disease which had already made their appearance, from the moment that he changed his sedentary habits for a more active life, became more and more pronounced and alarming. He continued, however, in full work till the close of the first term in the academic year

1861–62. At the beginning of the winter vacation, he was induced to seek relief by a change of scene and surroundings; and he visited his brother at Thurlow, Penn. Here his disease advanced rapidly to a fatal issue. After an attack in which his death was expected from moment to moment, he seemed for a little while convalescent. On the first day of the new term, I received a letter from him, dictated, as I afterward learned, when respiration and utterance were intermittent and painful, telling me that, as he had lain at the point of death, he had thought much of three students, who, otherwise without reproach, had received severe sentences from the Faculty for complicity in a serious hazing affair,[1] and begging, in the name of the Infinite Love to which he was looking in the grateful hope of renewed life, that the Faculty would remit the remaining portion of their sentence. On that evening, as the senior member of the Faculty, I presided at the regular meeting, read his letter, and obtained the desired vote. I had hardly reached my home when I received a telegram announcing his death.

Mr. Felton was the most generous of men. He was even false to his own reputation in his unstinted kindness to others. No one ever applied to him for aid in literary labor, without receiving all that he

[1] Mr. Felton took strong ground against the barbarous practice of hazing, made the most earnest efforts possible for its suppression and for the detection of those concerned in it, and regarded its extirpation as absolutely essential to the well-being and fair standing of the college.

asked and more. He would put aside work of his own which he wanted to finish, to look up authorities, furnish materials, revise manuscripts, or correct proof, for persons whom he knew only as applicants for his kind offices, and whose experience of them was apt to be so reported as constantly to increase the number of his clients. Had he given for his own fame the labor that he contributed to fame in which he had no share, he might have had more admirers, though fewer grateful friends.

With a temperament that might have seemed pliant, he had the impregnable defence and the unfailing guidance of a true, quick, sensitive, and discriminating conscience. We who knew him from his boyhood could recall, when he went from us, not an act or a word which we would wish to erase from our remembrance of him. His force of character, hidden on ordinary occasions by his gentle, sunny mien, was adequate for difficult emergencies, for painful duty, for reluctant severity. His character was founded on well-matured Christian faith and principle. He was unfeignedly reverent and devout, gave to the ordinances of religion his constant attendance and earnest advocacy, and sought in Jesus Christ his rule of life and his hope of immortality.

As regards literary labor, Mr. Felton contributed more than his share to various works, in which he was a joint author or editor with men of kindred tastes; and he published editions of several Greek works, with introductions and notes, for college use. He wrote many valuable articles for reviews and for "Appleton's Cyclopædia." He published many lectures and addresses, all of them, though ephemeral in form, elaborate in preparation, and worthy of more than a pamphlet's transitory life. But the works that do him the greatest honor were those published after his death, of which, as his friend of many years' standing, I undertook the editorship. One of these works is "Familiar Letters from Europe," which were written with no thought of publication, yet needed but a penstroke here and there to make them perfect as a record of travel; and the other, "Greece, Ancient and Modern." This last comprises in two octavo volumes four courses of lectures before the Lowell Institute. The chirography of a large part of these lectures showed that they were written in haste, often at the last moment before delivery; and I thought it desirable to verify the numerous references to, and translations from, Greek authors. But this work was almost needless. The materials were in great part such as originally required elaborate research; yet they must have been so familiar to him as to be at his free and full command on the stress of the passing moment.

SETH SWEETSER.

(1827.)

Dr. Sweetser seemed younger to me when I last saw him, a septuagenarian, crippled by chronic rheumatism, than when, as a member of the Junior class in college, he occupied the room under mine in Hollis. In college he seemed old, and certainly took no part even in the innocent juvenilities that made no small portion of the zest of student-life. He was then destined for the ministry, and his destiny was unconcealed. But there was nothing in his manners or intercourse that was not modest, unobtrusive, and kind. He was grave without austerity, sedate without gloom. He had the unqualified respect of his classmates and of all who knew him; and we were perfectly aware that he was then a man of mature character, of sincere self-consecration, and of lofty purpose. He was tutor for two years. His first settlement as a minister was, if I remember aright, at Hallowell, Me.; but the greater part of his life was spent as pastor of a church in Worcester, where he was beloved and honored by the whole community. A Calvinist of the old school, he was genial in his relations with those of widely differing faiths, and that not from mere good nature, but from his breadth of sympathy and largeness of heart. He gave his strong support and efficient aid to every institution and enterprise which he deemed conducive to the general well-being. He was intimately associated with the late Mr. Salisbury in the oversight and management of the Free Institute of Industrial Science, and continued to take part in its administration, even after he was no longer capable of public clerical duties. He was for many years one of the overseers of Harvard College, and never ceased to regard his *Alma Mater* with the love of a loyal son. The last few years of his life were a season of physical inability and suffering, which he bore with a cheerfulness and resignation that evinced how truly the religion of which he had been the minister had incorporated itself in his own heart and life. He died in 1878.

GEORGE STILLMAN HILLARD.

(1828.)

Mr. Hillard, whose name occurs in the list of proctors, had, on graduating, the first appointment at Commencement, and, if not really the first, was undoubtedly the second, scholar in his class. His life seemed in many respects eminently successful; but he was unrestingly ambitious, and thus had much of the air and manner of a disappointed man. In the legal profession he had a high reputation, held several offices of trust and honor, and was for some time one of the editors of "The Jurist." He was at different times in the government of the city of Boston and a member of both branches of the State Legislature. In literature he distinguished himself, both as an editor and as an author: and his "Six

Months in Italy" has and merits a place among the best itineraries of its kind; that is, among records, not merely of travel, but of æsthetic and artistical observation, description, and criticism. His writings, if collected, would make many volumes; and I doubt whether he ever wrote any thing, unless on some subject of transient interest, that was not worth preserving.

HENRY SWASEY McKEAN.

(1828.)

MR. McKEAN was for five years Latin tutor, and was afterward a librarian in New York. He was a man of accurate and elegant scholarship, of refined taste, and pure character. I was very intimate with him during my tutorship, but saw him only once for a few minutes afterward. His friendship was among the many which I have been forced to drop, but would, had distances been more easily overcome, have deemed it a great privilege to retain.

JAMES FREEMAN CLARKE.

(1829.)

I NAME him because his name is among the proctors; but I trust that it will be long before some chronicler who shall succeed me will be at liberty to commemorate his invaluable services to religion, to his country, and to his race.

BENJAMIN ROBBINS CURTIS.

(1829.)

JUDGE CURTIS, too, was a proctor. I had no intimacy with him, and, therefore, have no personal recollections of him. But, as a Massachusetts man, I feel proud of his record at the bar and on the bench, and, not the least, of his dissenting opinion in the Dred Scott case; while I am well aware that in the relations of home and of society he merited only unqualified respect, honor, and love.

SAMUEL ADAMS DEVENS.

(1829.)

MR. DEVENS, who was a proctor for a year or two, is an early friend of mine, whose life-work as a Christian minister was cut short midway by failure of health, but whose heart is none the less in his profession, and who is held in dear esteem by those whose fellow-worker he would gladly be.

JOEL GILES.

(1829.)

MR. GILES was tutor in the department of philosophy for three years, and, after Dr. Hedge's resignation, had the entire work of the department in his hands. As his fellow-tutor, I became intimate with him, and held him in high regard. He was grave and serious in deportment, as thoroughly versed in the subjects under his charge as a man of his age could well be, and in every respect fitted for a permanent place in the college Faculty. It was said, though I know not that he ever said, that he expected an appointment as professor. Certain it is that he did not commence the study of law till he resigned his tutorship, five years after graduating. He was a lawyer in Boston for forty-five years, held a high position for learning and ability, and had a large business as chamber counsel, without often appearing at the bar. It may have been strong religious sympathies rather than disaffection for any supposed neglect on the part of his own college, that brought him into close relations with Amherst College, in which he showed a great interest in his lifetime, and to which he left a considerable legacy. I was in daily and pleasant intercourse with him during my tutorship, but never saw him afterward; and when, a year or two ago, Mr. Vinton showed me a photograph of him, from which he was going to paint a portrait for Amherst College, I recognized not a single feature or trait that reminded me of my early friend.

BENJAMIN PEIRCE.

(1829.)

Professor Peirce's name appeared in fifty-four Annual Catalogues of the college. He died at the beginning of his fiftieth year of continuous service as tutor and professor, — a term equalled by no other college officer, except by Tutor Flynt, whose term of office was fifty-five years.

There was no faint promise of Professor Peirce's eminence in his parentage. His father, the librarian who has already been commemorated in these pages, was distinguished, not only for superior scholarship, but for a mind which, in its definiteness of conception and accuracy of statement, was potentially mathematical; though I know not whether his pursuits were ever in that direction. His mother belonged to a family remarkable for ability and attainments; and her brother, Rev. Dr. Ichabod Nichols, who was second to no man of his time in vigorous thought, lofty ideality, and kindling fervor of utterance, possessed also a rare love for mathematical study and investigation, was for four years mathematical tutor, and would probably have been a successful candidate for the professorship in that department, but for his preference for the pulpit.

While Benjamin Peirce the younger was still an undergraduate, his friend and fellow-townsman, Dr. Bowditch, employed the young scholar to read the proofs of his translation of Laplace's "Méchanique Céleste," and predicted that he would become the first mathematician of his age. It was said that in the class-room he not infrequently gave demonstrations that were not in the text-book, but were more direct, summary, or purely scientific than those in the lesson of the day. College-classes were then farther apart than they are now; but even in our senior year we listened, not without wonder, to the reports that came up to our elevated platform of this wonderful freshman, who was going to carry off the highest mathematical honors of the University. On graduating, he went to Northampton as a teacher in Mr. Bancroft's Round-Hill School, and returned to Cambridge in 1831 as tutor. The next year the absence of Professor Farrar in Europe left him at the head of the mathematical department, which he retained till his death,[1] the following year receiving his appointment as professor; while Mr. Farrar on his return was still unable to take charge of class-instruction.

For the academic year 1832–1833, I, as tutor, divided the mathematical instruction with Mr. Peirce, though, as we moved ostensibly side by side through the year's curriculum, it was certainly *passibus hand æquis*. He took to himself the instruction of the freshmen. The instruction of the other three classes we shared, each of us taking two of the four sections into which the class was divided, and interchanging our sections every fortnight. During that year I heard the freshmen recite in history, so that we both had under our tuition in the same year every student in college, — an arrangement which has probably not been repeated since. At that time a strictly mathematical course was a part of the required work for the first three years, while a *quasi* mathematical treatise on astronomy was studied for the first term in the senior year. In one respect I was Mr. Peirce's

[1] Professor James Mills Peirce, for the last ten years of his father's life, relieved him of much of the labor and responsibility that naturally fell to the head of the department.

superior, solely because I was so very far his inferior. I am certain that I was the better instructor of the two. The course in the sophomore and junior years, embracing a treatise on the Differential Calculus, with references to the calculus in the text-books on mechanics and other branches of mixed mathematics, was hardly within the unaided grasp of some of our best scholars; and, though no student dared to go to a tutor's room by daylight, it was no uncommon thing for one to come furtively in the evening to ask his teacher's aid in some difficult problem or demonstration. For this purpose resort was had to me more frequently than to my colleague, and often by students who belonged for the fortnight to one of his sections. The reason was obvious. No one was more cordially ready than he to give such help as he could; but his intuition of the whole ground was so keen and comprehensive, that he could not take cognizance of the slow and tentative processes of mind by which an ordinary learner was compelled to make his step-by-step progress. In his explanations he would take giant strides; and his frequent "You see" indicated what he saw clearly, but that of which his pupil could get hardly a glimpse. I, on the other hand, though fond of mathematical study, was yet so far from being a proficient in the more advanced parts of the course, that I studied every lesson as patiently and thoroughly as any of my pupils could have done. I, therefore, knew every short step of the way that they would be obliged to take, and could lead them in the very footsteps which I had just trodden before them.

Our year's work was on the whole satisfactory, and yet I think that we were both convinced that the Differential Calculus ought not to have been a part of a prescribed course. There was a great deal of faltering and floundering, even among else good scholars; and one young man, whose promise of a brilliant literary career was cut short by early death, and who was really very ambitious as a student, was excused from that part of the course on the ground of manifest and proved incapacity. Our examinations at that time were *viva voce*, in the presence of a committee of reputed experts in each several department. We shrank from the verdict of our special committee in no part of our work except the Calculus. As the day approached for the examination in that branch, we were solicitous that Robert Treat Paine, who was on the committee, should not be present; for we supposed him to be the only member of the committee who was conversant with the Calculus. He did not come, and we were glad. We had done our best, the class did its best; and, if there were defects and shortcomings, there was certainly no one present who could detect them. But a year or two before his death I told Mr. Paine of our hopes and fears on that occasion; and he replied, "I am entirely ignorant of the Calculus, and have not even the faintest conception of what it means."

had for his pupils only young men who were prepared for profounder study than ever entered into a required course, or a regularly planned curriculum; but he never before taught so efficiently, or with results so worthy of the mind and heart and soul, which he always put into his work. His students were inflamed by his fervor, and started by him on the eager pursuit of the eternal truth of God, of which mathematical signs and quantities are the symbols. He also did much for the instruction of a larger public, in several courses of lectures before the Lowell Institute, which are worthy of emphatic remembrance for such a union as no one else, so far as I know, has ever achieved, of close scientific reasoning, bold and universe-sweeping speculation, poetic fancy, creative imagination, and profound religious faith and reverence. In these lectures, he showed, as he always felt with adoring awe, that the mathematician enters, as none else can, into the intimate thought of God. This was his pervading consciousness, and it gave tone to his life-work and to his whole life. He was a theist and a Christian. Conversant with the various phases of scientific unbelief, and familiar with the historic grounds of scepticism, he maintained through life an unshaken belief in the Supreme Creator, and in his self-revelation in Jesus Christ. As this belief should have made him, he was pure, upright, and faithful; and we who knew him from his boyhood till his death knew of him only what was worthy of our love, admiration, and reverence.

his favor. He was ostracised from all intercourse with his class in general, and the other classes sympathized with the freshmen. This state of things lasted to the end of the year, how much longer I do not know; but the young man's name is in the Triennial Catalogue, and it seems to me that he could not have lived through three more years like his first. Robbins, as the schoolmate of this youth, knew him well, and, rightly, I have no doubt, believed him innocent and honorable; and he alone, or almost alone, assumed the defence and advocacy of his persecuted friend, and for a time shared in his unpopularity. That in what he deemed the cause of truth and right he thus, in his early youth, "made himself of no reputation," shows that he had already enlisted in the sacred service to which his life was consecrated.

Mr. Robbins held a high rank in a class which had an unusual number of men who afterward attained distinguished celebrity. After graduating, he received an appointment as usher in the Boston Latin School, in which he showed himself an excellent teacher, and — what was then a rare achievement — succeeded in maintaining good order in his class without the use of the rod or the ferule, — the only exception being a case of wanton cruelty, in which he inflicted deservedly severe punishment for the sake of its prevenient influence with his class. At the end of the year he entered the Divinity School; and, at the latest, midway in his course, if not earlier, Rev. Henry Ware, junior, set his eyes upon him as the minister of the church in Boston of which he had been pastor, and from which Mr. Emerson had recently withdrawn. The parish, as I believe, under Mr. Ware's advice, waited for Mr. Robbins, and, after hearing him preach as a candidate the then normal number of times, invited him to become their pastor. The church edifice was far down Hanover Street, which was then one of the most quiet streets in the city, with many substantial dwellings occupied by families of the highest respectability, some of them inheriting the names and homes of those who had lived there in the time of the Mathers. That quarter of the city, then containing some eight or nine Protestant houses of worship, was, however, rapidly changing its population; and when, ten years later, a bare majority voted to build a new church on the same spot, all who did not so vote were perfectly aware that the necessity for removal was even then imminent. The society, in fact, almost made the circuit of the city, worshiping in Bedford Street and in two different buildings on Tremont Street, before erecting its present church on Boylston Street.

Dr. Robbins's style as a preacher was simple, easy, flowing, and elegant. His delivery was natural, and therefore graceful, his voice and gesture taking with prompt elasticity the mould of his thought. He was a devoted pastor, and made himself very dear in the homes of his people, especially in their seasons of trial and sorrow, when they derived from him equally tender sympathy and the resources of Christian support and consolation. He had a vein of poetry which yielded little ore, indeed, but that little golden. He wrote many hymns; and, toward the close of life, he was in the constant habit of dictating in a metrical form the thoughts of peace and hope which were unspeakably precious to him. One of his hymns, commencing, —

> "Lo! the day of rest declineth;
> Gather fast the shades of night,"

is found in almost all American, and in some transatlantic, hymnals. Dr. Robbins's daughter, on her home-passage from England, joined a group of passengers who were singing hymns one Sunday afternoon. An aged Scotch Presbyterian minister went into his state-room, and brought out a hymn-and-tune book, asking those who were leading in the music to sing from it what he regarded as the sweetest hymn he knew, and the sweetest tune. It was this hymn of Dr. Robbins, set to the tune of Bedford Street, which was composed expressly for it when the temporary home of the author's church was in Bedford Street.

Dr. Robbins had to a large extent the taste and talent of an antiquary; and, had it not been for his paramount interest in his higher calling, he might very probably have made historical research his life-work. As pastor of the Second Church in Boston, he had repeated occasions, at anniversary and commemorative epochs, to explore the obscure portions of Boston's early ecclesiastical history; and, with the Mathers as his predecessors, there was no little space of controverted biographical ground for his investigation. Such work of this kind as he did was so well done, that his associates in it would have been glad to have it more. As long as he could be he was an active member of the Massachusetts Historical Society, for several years a member of its council, and co-editor with the late George Livermore of the first two volumes of its "Proceedings." He also made valuable contributions to various literary and religious periodicals.

Dr. Robbins, several years before his death, met with an accident which was probably the cause of his loss of sight. From that time, darkness gathered over him by slow but sure stages, with no hopeful intermission. He worked while he was yet able, cheerfully and earnestly; and when the shadows became so dense that he could guide neither his pen nor his steps, he submitted, not as to the inevitable, but as to the hidden mercy of a loving Providence. I saw him often during his blindness. Indeed, I met him every month at the sessions of a clerical club, composed of clergymen of six different denominations; and to the last, he bore his part in our discussions, while he won the sincere respect, affection, and sympathy of all the members. He died just at the time when longer life must have been divested of the employments and recreations which had been his solace; and he was thus relieved from the prolonged consciousness of helpless imbecility. His death occurred on the 11th of September, 1862. I was absent from the country at that time, and it was a season when many of his friends were absent from Boston. Special commemorative services were postponed till the last evening of that year.

THOMAS HOPKINSON.

(1830.)

THOMAS HOPKINSON rather wrought out for himself than received a liberal education. Conscious of the need of high culture, and of the capacity to utilize it, he worked his way through difficulties that would have broken down a feebler will. He prepared himself for college, and acquired all of Latin and Greek demanded for admission, in a single year; and while in college, though not without kind friends, his vigorous self-help did much more for him than was done for him beside. He had the one advantage of mature age and self-discipline, but every thing else seemed against him; though, in fact, obstacles surmounted[1] are always of immeasurable service. He graduated at the head of his class, and would have delivered the usual English oration, which was the crowning Commencement honor, but for a disabling attack of illness. He was able to attend a part of the services of the day, but not to

[1] Obstacles are stumbling-blocks, fatal to him who stumbles upon them, enfeebling and discouraging to him who creeps round them; while he who *sur-mounts* them, mounts upon them, and stands upon a higher plane.

walk in the procession, or to take his seat with his class. I well remember the disappointment of that day. Commencement and the first scholar of the class meant more then, and were regarded with very much more general interest, than now; and Hopkinson's college career, so honorable in its noble self-reliance, was largely known. Thus, the president's *Hopkinson necessario ab est* was not very graciously received by the audience.

Mr. Hopkinson studied law at the Cambridge Law School, but not long enough to receive his degree, the conferment of which was then a question of time, not of merit. During this period, he served as proctor. He settled as a lawyer at Lowell, where he lived for many years. He there held various offices in the city government, and represented the city in the House of Representatives, and the county in the Senate. Offices of trust gravitated naturally toward him, and he occupied several important financial positions. In 1848 he was appointed judge of the Court of Common Pleas; and, had he retained the office, no man was more likely than he to have filled some early vacancy on the Supreme Bench. But at the end of a year he resigned his judgeship, to assume the presidency of the Boston and Worcester Railroad, which he filled till his death in 1856. In the memorial volume, published by his class, it is well said of him, —

"He was a man who never knowingly wronged another, but was always ready with hand, purse, or brain to assist those in need and trouble; a man who never spared himself in the performance of his duties, nor exacted too much from those in his employ. He left behind him a host of loving and devoted friends, and to his children a reputation without a stain."

Mr. Hopkinson's wife, a daughter of John Prentiss of Keene, N.H., a woman of rare gifts and graces of mind and heart, survived him for twenty-seven years. Of his two sons, Francis Custis (H. U., 1859), a young man of beautiful promise, died in the service of his country, in the war of the Rebellion; the other, John Prentiss (H. U., 1861), lives in the service of his country, as a classical teacher, second to none in the thoroughness of his work, and the worth of his influence. Of Mr. Hopkinson's two daughters, one is happily married to a son of my classmate Goodwin; and as for the other, the friends of Harvard College, and of its president, can never be unmindful of the hospitality and kindness of Mrs. Eliot.

CHARLES EAMES.

(1831.)

In the early summer of 1832 I took possession as proctor, for a few weeks, of the room in the north-west corner of Massachusetts, which for some reason Charles Eames had just vacated. I never saw him afterward. He was the first scholar of his class, and was regarded as a man of unlimited power of acquisition, and of marked ability as a public speaker, but not as largely possessed of creative or inventive mental capacity. He was a prominent member of the Democratic party, and was appointed by Mr. Polk as commissioner to the Hawaiian Islands for the negotiation of a treaty, and by Mr. Pierce as minister to Venezuela. At different times he assumed the editorial charge of leading newspapers in Nashville and in Washington. For the last few years of his life he practised law in Washington, and was distinguished for his legal learning, especially in international law. During the war of the Rebellion he had the professional management of many important prize cases, and was regarded as among the greatest admiralty lawyers in the country. He died in 1867.

SUPPLEMENTARY CHAPTER.

HARVARD COLLEGE SIXTY YEARS AGO.

THE last sixty years can hardly have wrought greater changes, whether superficial or radical, anywhere else than in Harvard College. In my time a student's room was remarkable chiefly for what it did not have, — for the absence of all appliances of elegance and comfort, I might almost say, of all tokens of civilization. The feather-bed — mattresses not having come into general use — was regarded as a valuable chattel; but ten dollars would have been a fair auction-price for all the other contents of an average room, which were a pine bedstead, wash-stand, table, and desk, a cheap rocking-chair, and from two to four other chairs of the plainest fashion, the bed furnishing seats when more were needed. I doubt whether any fellow-student of mine owned a carpet. A second-hand-furniture dealer had a few defaced and threadbare carpets, which he leased at an extravagant price to certain Southern members of the senior class; but even Southerners, though reputed to be fabulously rich, did not aspire to this luxury till the senior year. Coal was just coming into use, and had hardly found its way into college. The students' rooms — several of the recitation-rooms as well — were heated by open wood-fires. Almost every room had, too, among its *transmittenda*, a cannon-ball supposed to have been derived from the arsenal, which on very cold days was heated to a red heat, and placed as a calorific radiant on a skillet, or on some extemporized metallic stand; while at other seasons it was often utilized by being rolled downstairs at such time as might most nearly bisect a proctor's night-sleep. Friction-matches — according to Faraday the most useful invention of our age — were not yet. Coals were carefully buried in ashes over night to start the morning fire; while in summer, as I have elsewhere said, the evening-lamp could be lighted only by the awkward, and often baffling, process of "striking fire" with flint, steel, and tinder-box.

The student's life was hard. Morning-prayers were in summer at six; in winter, about half an hour before sunrise in a bitterly cold chapel. Thence half of each class passed into the several recitation-rooms in the same building (University Hall), and three-quarters of an hour later the bell rang for a second set of recitations, including the remaining half of the students. Then came breakfast, which in the college commons consisted solely of coffee, hot rolls, and butter, except when the members of a mess had succeeded in pinning to the nether surface of the table, by a two-pronged fork, some slices of meat from the previous day's dinner. Between ten and twelve every student attended another recitation or a lecture. Dinner was at half-past twelve, — a meal not deficient in quantity, but by no means appetizing to those who had come from neat homes and well-ordered tables. There was another recitation in the afternoon, except on Saturday; then evening prayers at six, or in winter at early twilight; then the evening meal, plain as the breakfast, with tea instead of coffee, and cold bread, of the consistency of wool, for the hot rolls. After tea the dormitories rang with song and merriment till the study-bell, at eight in winter, at nine in summer, sounded the curfew for fun and frolic, proclaiming dead silence throughout the college premises, under penalty of a domiciliary visit from the officer of the entry, and, in case of a serious offence, of private or public admonition.

This was the life for five days of the week. On Sundays all the students were required to be in residence here, not excepting even those whose homes were in Boston; and all were required to attend worship twice each day at the college chapel. On Saturday alone was there permission to leave Cambridge, absence from town at any other time being a punishable offence. This weekly liberty was taken by almost every member of college, Boston being the universal resort; though seldom otherwise than on foot, the only public conveyance then being a two-horse stage-coach, which ran twice a day. But the holiday could not be indefinitely prolonged. The students who were not present at evening prayers were obliged by law to register their names with the regent before nine o'clock, under a heavy penalty, which was seldom or never incurred; for the regent's book was kept by his freshman,[1] who could generally be coaxed or bribed to "take no note of time."

The price of board in commons was a dollar and three-quarters, or, as was then the uniform expression, "ten and sixpence." The dining-rooms were on the first floor of University Hall. College officers and graduates had a table on an elevated platform at the head of each room, and the students occupied the main floor in messes of from eight to ten. The round windows opening into the halls, and the shelves set in them, still remaining in some of these rooms, were designed for the convenience of waiters in bringing dishes from the kitchen in the basement. That kitchen, cooking for about two hundred persons, was the largest culinary establishment of which the New-England mind then had knowledge or conception, and it attracted curious visitors from the whole surrounding country; while the students felt in large part remunerated for coarse fare and rude service by their connection with a feeding-place that possessed what seemed to them world-wide celebrity. They were not the only dependants upon the college kitchen, but shared its viands with a half-score or more of swine, whose sties were close in the rear of

[1] Every parietal officer had freshmen living under him, who were subject to his order for college errands, and some of whom, like the regent's freshman, performed important services, and received an adequate compensation.

the building, and with rats of abnormal size that had free quarters with the pigs. Board of a somewhat better quality was to be had at private houses for a slight advance on the college price; while two or three of the professors received select boarders at the then enormous charge of three dollars a week. This last arrangement, except when known to be peremptorily insisted on by some anxious parent, exposed a student to suspicion and unpopularity; and, if one of a professor's boarders received any college honor, it was uniformly ascribed to undue influence catered for on the one side, and exerted on the other, in consequence of this domestic arrangement.

From what has just been said, it may be inferred that the relations between the Faculty and the students were regarded, as has been already intimated, on one side at least, as those of mutual hostility. The students certainly considered the Faculty as their natural enemies. There existed between the two parties very little of kindly intercourse, and that little generally secret. If a student went unsummoned to a teacher's room, it was almost always by night. It was regarded as a high crime by his class for a student to enter a recitation-room before the ringing of the bell, or to remain to ask a question of the instructor; and even one who was uniformly first in the class-room would have had his way to Coventry made easy. The professors, as well as the parietal officers, performed police duty as occasion seemed to demand; and in case of a general disturbance, which was not infrequent, the entire Faculty were on the chase for offenders, — a chase seldom successful; while their unskilled manœuvres in this uncongenial service were wont to elicit, not so much silent admiration, as shouts of laughter and applause, which they strove in vain to trace to their source.

The recitations were mere hearings of lessons, without comment or collateral instruction. They were generally heard in quarter-sections of a class, the entire class containing from fifty to sixty members. The custom was to call on every student in the section at every recitation. Each teacher was supposed to have some system, according to which he arranged the order of his daily calls. Some, like Dr. Popkin, openly adopted the direct, some the inverse, alphabetical order, some the two alternately. As for the key to the order adopted by the others respectively, there were, generally, conflicting theories, the maintenance of which brought into play a keenness of calculation and a skilful manipulation of data fully adequate to the solving of deeply involved algebraic equations. Of course, the endeavor — not always unsuccessful — was to determine what part of a lesson it was necessary for each individual student to prepare.

The leading feature of the college at that time was the rich provision made for courses of lectures. It may be doubted whether so many lecturers of an exceptionally high order have ever, at any one time, been brought together in the service of an American college. We had courses on physics and astronomy by Professor Farrar, of whose surpassing eloquence I have already spoken; on technology, by the late Dr. Bigelow; on anatomy, by Dr. John Collins Warren; on hygiene, by Dr. Jackson; on law, by Chief Justice Parker; on French and Spanish literature, by Professor Ticknor; on the canon of the New Testament, by the elder Dr. Ware. It is my belief, that, with the then existing materials and means of knowledge, neither of these courses admitted of any essential improvement; and several of the lecturers had extended fame as speakers and writers in the outside world. By far the largest part of our actual instruction was that of the lecture-room, where it was our custom to take copious notes, which were afterward written out in full for our permanent use and benefit.

As regards the amount of study and of actual attainment, it was, I think, much greater with the best scholars of each class, much less with those of a lower grade, than now. I doubt whether such students as used to constitute the fourth quarter of a class could now reach the sophomore year. A youth who was regular in his habits, and who made some sort of an answer, however wide of the mark, at half of his recitations, commonly obtained his degree, though his college-life might have been interpolated by an annual three-months' suspension for negligence. But the really good scholar gave himself wholly to his work. He had no distractions, no outside society, no newspapers, no legal possibility of an evening in Boston, no probable inducement to spend an hour elsewhere than within college-walls, and not even easy access to the college library. Consequently, there remained for him nothing but hard study; and there were some in every class whose hours of study were not less than sixty a week.

The range of study was much less extensive than now. Natural history did not then even profess to be a science, and received very little attention. Chemistry, under auspices which one does not like to recall, occupied, and utterly wasted, a small portion of the senior year. French and Spanish were voluntary studies, or rather recreations; for the recitation-room of the kind-hearted septuagenarian, who had these languages in charge, was frequented more for amusement than for any thing that was taught or learned. Italian and German were studied in good earnest by a very few volunteers. There was a great deal of efficient work in the department of philosophy; and the writing of English could not have been cared for more faithfully, judiciously, and fruitfully, than by Professor Channing. But the chief labor and the crowning honor of successful scholarship were in mathematics and the classics. The mathematical course extended through the entire four years; embracing the differential calculus, the mathematical treatment of all departments of physical science then studied, and a thoroughly mathematical treatise on astronomy.[1] In Greek and Latin, the aim, as has been already stated, was not so much to determine grammatical inflections and construction, as to reach the actual meaning of the author in hand, and to render his thought into perspicuous and elegant English. This aim was attained, I think, to a high degree in Latin; and with the faithful and searching study of the Latin text, there grew up inevitably the sort of instinctive knowledge of Latin grammar, which one conversant with the best English writers acquires of English grammar, without formal study. Such grammatical tact and skill were acquired by a respectable number of Latin scholars in every class; and the number was by no means small of those who then formed a life-long taste for Latin literature, and the capacity of reading it with all desirable ease and fluency. Greek, for reasons given in my sketch of Dr. Popkin, was studied with much greater difficulty, and, when with similar, with much less satisfactory and valuable results. The best scholars were often discouraged in the pursuit of knowledge under hindrances so grave, and had resort to contraband methods of preparation, which required little labor, and were of no permanent benefit.

These are a few of the many illustrations which I might give of the contrast between the Harvard of to-day and that of sixty years ago; and they may

[1] Gummere's, afterward replaced by Farrar's almost purely descriptive treatise.

render some help in answering the question whether the former days were better than these; while they may not altogether satisfy the class of persons characterized by those eminently graphic verses, —

> "Qui redit ad fastos, et virtutem æstimat annis,
> Miraturque nihil nisi quod Libitina sacravit."

It remains for me to give some account of the college buildings, as they were in my time.

The principal buildings were within the college-yard, then unenclosed, and extending but a few feet to the rear of University Hall. Within this area there were seven buildings, all still standing, and but little changed in their exterior aspect.

The pride of college architecture, then comparatively new, was University Hall. Its basement was devoted to culinary and menial uses. The lower story had four apartments, built as dining-rooms, for the four classes severally. Whether the two inner rooms were ever so used, I do not know; but I think not. Of the two other rooms, one was occupied by the senior and sophomore, the other by the junior and freshman, classes. By this arrangement each pair of adjacent classes, always supposed to hold relations of mutual antagonism, were fed apart, and had different doors of entrance and egress. The chapel — its site still marked by long, arched windows — filled the space between the two entry-ways and staircases in the second and third stories. There were seats on one side for the seniors and sophomores, on the other for the juniors and freshmen, with different entrance-doors, so that there might be no hostile collision on the stairs. In front of the pulpit was a stage for the public declamations and exhibitions, and on each side of it a raised sentry-box, occupied at daily prayers by a professor or tutor on the watch for misdemeanors. Opposite the pulpit was the organ, with a double row of raised seats on each side, — one for the choir, the other for parietal officers and graduates. There were two side-galleries, where were pews for the families of the professors and of a few persons more or less remotely connected with the college. At the southern end of the building, where are now the offices of the president and the dean, there were in the second story two rooms, commonly called the corporation rooms. That in the rear contained such models and apparatus as were used by Dr. Bigelow in his lectures on technology, with settees in sufficient number to accommodate his classes, the average number of a class being then less than sixty. The front room no undergraduate ever saw. It was opened only at two of the three public exhibitions, when the corporation made their semi-annual official visit to the college, and dined in that room with their invited guests. At a later period dinners were served there for committees of examination. Above these rooms were two recitation-rooms, which, with four in the second and third stories on the northern end, sufficed for the regular daily recitations in philosophy, mathematics, Latin, and Greek. There was originally, on a level with the lower story of this building, a roofed piazza, which was removed during a period of rigid discipline, as it was said, to check the "grouping" of students, which used to be a penal offence, two having been a sufficient number to constitute a group; while, in at least one instance, an extra-zealous proctor reported a solitary student as evidently waiting to be joined by another, and thus offering himself as a nucleus for a group.

Harvard Hall had then the same bell that hangs in it now. There was also connected with the bell a clock which struck the hour, and which presented two dial-faces, — the same clock, which, still the property of the college, gives note of time from the steeple of the First Parish Church. The upper story of the building was devoted to the library, which filled the western, and had begun to overflow into the eastern, apartment. In the lower story the western room contained such apparatus as belonged to the departments of physics and astronomy, with very well arranged seats for Professor Farrar's classes. The eastern room was called the mineralogical cabinet, and had in it a considerable quantity of rock, but few specimens of value, having been depleted rather than enriched during several previous years.

Holden Chapel had been floored over, midway, so as to make two stories. On the lower floor was the chemical laboratory, with an adjacent lecture-room; in the second story, the anatomical cabinet, with a lecture-room lighted from above, cheerful, airy, and by far the most beautiful apartment then appertaining to the college.

There were on college-grounds four dormitories,— Massachusetts, Hollis, Stoughton, and Holworthy. The first three of these were arranged substantially on the same plan, each with thirty-two rooms, of which two in each building were occupied by tutors or proctors; one or two in Massachusetts, and one in Hollis, used as modern-language recitation-rooms; one in Stoughton, assigned to a scientific society of undergraduates; those on the lower floor reserved for freshmen, and the rest allotted to applicants belonging to the three upper classes, in accordance with some numerical gradation of claims, the key to which was lodged, if anywhere, in the steward's inmost consciousness. The lower rooms and the rooms of the parietal officers were fitted with blinds. These last were also provided with a sufficiency of plain, substantial furniture, of a quality not much inferior to what would be deemed fitting for a servant's room at the present day. They also had bedrooms built over the entrance-hall, and so had the third and fourth story rooms above them. In these tutors' rooms there was one fixture which, as already obsolescent in the knowledge of living men, deserves special commemoration. They were all furnished with genuine Franklin stoves, said to have been almost coeval with the invention. I doubt whether there still exists a Franklin stove. The stove that bears the name is simply an iron fireplace, which required for its invention no scientific genius. Franklin's stove — I have read the description as he wrote it — has two iron backs, with an air-chamber between them, an opening into that chamber from the external air, and an aperture from that chamber on each side of the stove, from which a current of heated air is poured into the room. This is, indeed, the germ of the hot-air furnace, which is simply a Franklin stove set in the cellar. I have had large experience with various descriptions of heating-apparatus, and I have never found ample heating-power, pure air, and economy of fuel, combined so efficiently as in Hollis No. 7, which I occupied as tutor. Holworthy had, in my time, but four stories (the fifth having been recently added), and twenty-four rooms, each, as now, with two bedrooms. Three of these rooms were occupied by college officers, the three under them by freshmen, the remaining eighteen by such seniors as had the highest numerical claim, in order to obtain which students often petitioned in the two previous years for rooms of the lowest grade; as, according to a commendably equitable rule, those who had had the most could claim the least. Justice in the assignment of rooms in successive years, which was certainly intended in the steward's allotment, was the more obligatory, inasmuch as the rents of college-rooms were equal, and the best room in Holworthy in the senior year was no more than an offset for a three-years' occupancy of the poorest rooms in Massachusetts.

The president's house, now called Wadsworth House, was within the college-yard. The president's study, or office, was where the printing-office now is; and his freshman occupied the room below.

On the present site of the First Parish Church, there were two old wooden buildings, one of three, and one of two, stories, which were designated in the catalogue as College House 1 and 2. In the lower story of one of these, there used to be a barber's shop, also a shop with a workroom in the rear, kept by two ladies of an impoverished branch of an old Cambridge family. This shop supplied such small articles of haberdashery as the students required: and they resorted to it for the mending, and even for the making, of apparel; for it was believed that the skill of the average country tailor was transcended by these experienced workwomen. They also had a lucrative investment in the gowns worn by students at exhibitions and on Commencement Day, for the use of which the fee was two or three dollars, according to the quality. The gowns were of the flimsiest texture and of scanty amplitude; and, as they were worn by a very considerable number of students four times a year, they must have paid six per cent. on a capital of at the least five thousand dollars. The lower story of the other College House was the seat of the then infant Law School. The upper stories of these buildings were occupied, in part, by undergraduates who could not get rooms within the college-yard; in great part, by certain ancient resident graduates who had become water-logged on their life-voyage, by preachers who could not find willing hearers, by men lingering on the threshold of professions for which they had neither the courage nor the capacity, notably, by Jonathan Peale Dabney, of whom my older readers need no description, and whom no descriptive power of mine could make conceivable to those who did not know him, — in fine, by such waifs of literary purlieus as in these faster days would be speedily blown away, and as since those old garrets were pulled down have found no shelter in Cambridge.

The only other buildings belonging to the University when I entered college, so far as I know, were the Botanic Garden house, — which has for many years been the home of Dr. Gray, — and the Medical College in Boston. Divinity Hall was erected while I was in college, and dedicated in the month in which I graduated.

INDEX.